AMISH CANNING AND PRESERVING COOKBOOK

FOR BEGINNERS

1200 Days of Delicious Recipes to Learn the Grandma's Secret to Water Bath

and Pressure Canning Meat, Vegetables and Much More

Maria Delice Leighton

Table of Contents

INTRODUCTION

Amish Canning and Preserving offers traditional recipes for fresh produce grown in the backyard. These methods are well known to the Amish and are essential to their large family structures and extensive gardens. Amish communities store food during the winter when the garden is no longer in production, and the crop has been harvested for a long time. For generations, Amish families have been preparing for the winter and spring seasons through canning, a method by which they seal food into glass jars to preserve it for future use.

Since the Amish do not use modern stoves and dishwashers to prepare their jars, they have maintained mainly the old canning traditions with some twists and turns. Amish women do not even use food processes to chop tomatoes, onions, and other sauce ingredients finely, so they do it all by hand, adding much time to the preparation work before the food can be put in the hot jars for processing. The Amish use to can meat as well as fruits and vegetables. The advantage of this practice is that when a meal must be prepared in winter, the meat is ready to be added to all recipes. No need to wait for the meat to simmer! It is particularly helpful if last-minute guests arrive just in time for dinner. The practice of canning has been transmitted from mother to daughter within the Amish community for generations. It is possible to enjoy authentic Amish canned products in their markets, such as fruit jams, preserves, vegetables, and other typical delights.

Preserving food is more than just a method to save money on grocery bills, store for the winter, or make charming culinary presents for occasions. Preserving food is also a technique to ensure that food will last longer. While it is possible that modern food preservation can indeed be every one of those qualities, it can also be a strategy to lessen the overall environmental impact by ensuring that you have access to foods that are grown or raised locally throughout the whole year. Statistics show that one in four households in the United States does home canning for personal use. Home canning is being revived in many households in the country because an increasing number of individuals have seen the benefits of eating locally.

Preparing preserves, jams, and jellies at home has become an exciting hobby for millions of people. In addition, it is a great way to save bucks and feel independent to make them whenever you need them or your mood strikes. Commercially available preserves, jams, relishes, etc., are costly compared to homemade versions and contain preservatives, additives, artificial colors, and chemicals.

One great advantage of homemade canning is that you can prepare it from fresh ingredients and ensure that what you consume is free of additives and preservatives. Another great advantage is that you can keep total control over ingredients' quantities; not everyone likes the same amount of sweetness or sourness in preserves and jams. This way, you can adjust the sugar quantity and savory ingredients, such as vinegar, lemon juice, etc., to suit your taste.

Homemade canning gives you another advantage of preparing them in small quantities; when you prepare them in small quantities, these canning recipes maintain their natural flavors. Short batches allow you to make different varieties every time and rotate them as per seasonal ingredients. It takes less space to store, and you can enjoy fresh batches by preparing them at shorter intervals. If it gets spoiled due to external environmental issues, the wastage amount is quite less.

Chapter 1:

What Is Canning?

Canning is an excellent method to preserve fruits and vegetables from the garden or farmer's market while they are still in season. It extends the bounty into the winter when local and seasonal items are limited.

Canning in water baths and pressure cookers warms the food and generates a vacuum seal in the jar, killing any germs that could develop. The vacuum seal will prevent air from getting into the preserved food, which might increase cell development and spoilage.

The term "canning" is a bit of a misnomer. Metal canning is no longer widely used in home canning as it is in industrial canning. Glass canning jars with appropriately constructed lids are the preferred preservation method.

Canning may be done in two ways: in a boiling water bath or a pressure canner. If you wish to preserve food in sealed jars at room temperature securely, you must understand the differences between the two ways. The easier of the two procedures is boiling water bath canning. It requires using a big, deep pot and canning jars with lids. The essential thing to remember about boiling water bath canning is that this technique is only safe for high-acid foods.

What do you mean by high-acid foods? Fruits, vinegar-based pickles (including chutneys), fruit-based sweet preserves such as jams and jellies, and tomatoes with extra acidity are high-acid foods. In order for the food to be adequately conserved in a boiling water bath, the pH of the food contained in the jars must be 4.6 or lower.

In a boiling water bath, jars containing any of those items may be safely processed. Besides pickled vegetables and stock for soup, all other foods, including meats and vegetables that aren't pickled, should always be prepared in a pressurized canner.

The food can be preserved longer with the use of heat processing in a boiling water bath, but this does not guarantee that the contents are safe to consume. The conclusion that can be drawn from this is that the acidity of the contents of each jar, as opposed to the heat of the processing, is what safely preserves the food when it is placed in a bath of boiling water. When used in conjunction with canning jars and lids, a water bath that is brought to a boil creates a vacuum seal that prevents mold from growing within the jars. When the jars are opened, they must be kept in the refrigerator, much like store-bought canned items.

You could come across old-fashioned methods for sealing your canning jars, such as flipping them upside down while the food inside is still hot or putting them in the oven. It is not a good idea! Although the jars may have sealed, there is no guarantee that a real vacuum has been formed.

Furthermore, the food within may not have reached the temperature of boiling water to the core using those ways. Canning periods (also known as processing times) are determined by the food's density and the jar's size, both of which influence how long it takes for all of the food to reach the temperature of the hot water in the surrounding area.

By canning, the shelf life of products can be increased significantly, and food remains edible for much longer than it ordinarily would.

Studies have found that canned foods are not lacking in the nutritional value that fresh foods have and sometimes even serve as healthier alternatives.

Chapter 2:
Types of Food Canning: The two Canning Methods

Canning can be done using either a water bath or under pressure. Both methods are described here. The kind of food you intend to preserve will, in most cases, determine which canning method you go with. Acidic foods work fine with the water bath canning technique. For others, such as vegetables and meats, you will want to invest in that pressure canner so you can follow that technique. You will want to use this technique when you are making relishes, jams, pickles, fruits, salsas, condiments, and vinegar.

Water-Bath Canning

For water bath canning, you are basically placing your food in a jar, wiping down the rims, affixing the lid to the jar, boiling the jars, and then removing them when it's safe. Here are more instructions for this canning method:

First, make sure your jars, lids, and bands work before you use them. Do not use jars that are chipped, scratched, or compromised in any way. You do not want them to break during the canning process. Wash your jars, lids, and bands in warm water with soap, and dry them. You don't have to do any excessive sterilization. As long as they are clean, you will be fine.

Heat the jars in hot water while you prepare the food. It should not be boiling water, and you do not have to cover the jars. Simply let them rest in a pot that is half-full with hot water. When you place hot food inside the jars, this will protect them from breaking because of the heat.

Prepare your recipe with whatever foods you plan to can. Remove your hot jar from the water, using a jar lifter. Fill the jars with your food, using a large spoon or a funnel. Keep an empty space of at least a half an inch at the top of each jar. You may get rid of any air bubbles in the meal by pressing down on it with a spoon or a spatula.

11

Wiping the top of the container with a moist cloth will remove any food residue that may have accumulated there. After applying the band as well as the lid, make sure it is secure.

Place the containers in a big pot full of water and make sure the water covers the jars fully before proceeding. Heat the water until it boils. Processing time will depend on your recipe.

Once it is finished, pull the containers & put them somewhere where they may warm up to room temperature. You will want to leave them undisturbed for at least 12 hours.

Pressure Canning

Pressure canning is the process of safely processing vegetables, fruits, meat, poultry, or fish by boiling them in hot water near the boiling point for an extended period. The resulting product must be under high enough pressure to kill microorganisms and force out the air before sealing it in a jar or other container with an airtight lid.

The high-pressure cooker cooks' food, allowing it to reach high cooking temperatures, which help to preserve the quality and consistency of the product for long shelf life.

The products of this process are shelf-stable without refrigeration. They can be stored on your shelf or in the basement of the house for long periods with no loss of quality or nutritional value.

The process that is used to sterilize foods is not the same one that is used to pasteurize foods. Pasteurization works by heating food for a short period, usually less than fifteen minutes, just enough time to destroy undesirable pathogens and contaminants, but not enough to kill all dangerous bacteria and create dangerous toxins. The difference between the two processes is that pasteurization is used to preserve milk, milk products, meat, vegetables, seafood, fresh fruit, and other raw food products. The process of pressure canning is used to preserve foods that are cooked or cured to prevent spoilage.

Pressure canning uses a double-boiler method much like the one used in the home kitchen for boiling water. A tight lid prevents pressure build up inside the pot and allows steam to escape quickly. The boiling water forces steam into jars for high-pressure processing. Vegetables are steamed or cooked in a sealed chamber at low heat for ten minutes or more to destroy any harmful microorganisms without cooking out their flavor.

Types Of Pressure Canners

There are two kinds of pressure canners: Dial gauge and weighted gauge. Many pressure-canning recipes will include two sets of instructions or pressures for each type.

Weighted Gauge Pressure Canner

This pressure canner has a weight attached to the steam valve. It is usually set at 5, 10, or 15 PSI. The steam is released when the temperature reaches this point. These canners are easy to control because they have a built-in steam regulator.

After reaching the desired temperature, turn down the heat until the weight moves about once per minute. This ensures the canner stays hot enough to process the food properly but does not blow steam off all the time.

My stove is between medium and low heat.

These canners are easy to use, as you don't need to watch them as much. They also maintain consistent pressure without the need for constant adjustments. There are only three settings available: 5, 10, or 15 PSI.

Dial Gauge Pressure Canner

You will need to be watching the dial on the top of a dial gauge canner to regulate pressure. You'll be required to adjust the heat so that the pressure in the canner doesn't drop below your desired level. This allows you to maintain a temperature intermediate (for example, 12 PSI), but this comes at the expense of your attention and time.

Canning is a good way to save money, but it is not worth spending an hour staring at a gauge.

You can use a dial gauge to pay close attention to the canner, listening for it to "jig" every minute. You can do other things with your hands and make the most of your time.

Water Bath Canning and Pressure Canning Differences

Canning can be intimidating and confusing, but there is no need to fear: Here we'll decode the differences between the water bath and pressure canning.

Water bath: Jars are placed in a huge pot of boiling water, and the water is left to boil for a predetermined period of time.

Pressure: The pot has a rubber seal around the upper edge so that when you heat it, air pressure builds up inside. This makes the food cook faster because the temperature gets hotter than it would in boiling water. It is also better for high-acid foods like fruits and tomatoes because they are processed at higher temperatures than lower-acid foods like vegetables.

Both water bath and pressure canning are A-Okay for acidic foods, but when it comes to high-acid foods, pressure-cooking is the only way to go.

Some people argue that the taste of home-canned tomatoes is better with a water bath. However, if you do it correctly, you can get equally good results with a pressure cooker.

The only difference between the two lies in what kind of food you are canning. The water bath is great for low-acid food like meat or vegetables, while pressure-cooking is ideal for high-acid food like tomatoes or fruit jellies/jams.

Chapter 3:
Learn How to Can Your Own Food at Home

Besides the reasons you want to preserve food, many people do not know about more specific and less known benefits. This will briefly outline and discuss these 'secret benefits' largely unknown throughout the food preservation world. Everyone knows that canning and preserving foods protect large quantities of food products over time. Some methods such as drying have been used for millennia. Canning and freezing are more recent and contemporary methods of food preservation.

Regardless of the technique, food preservation's 'secret benefits' apply to it. One of the 'secret benefits' is that food preservation permits you to have a store occupied with quality diets for a long period. How is this 'secret benefit?' wait a minute; we have already covered this, have not we? The reality is that having a stock of healthy, quality foods for a long period serves as a buffer against any economic downturns that could lead to food shortages.

However, many individuals seldom have this thought at the back of their minds when they decide they want to preserve foods.

Being safe is always a good thing. When fresh food is both abundant and inexpensive, it is in your best interest to take advantage of the situation.

Preserving food is also convenient. If you are busy or are lacking some more time with your family, you will be surprised at how much more time on your hands you will have. You will also be able to build a sense of confidence in yourself as you build confidence in the different ingredients in the foods you plan to preserve.

You have full control over everything. More so, you have complete control over the process, compared to the foods with specific ingredients you are forced to buy from the store. This 'secret benefit' could be seeing oneself as a pro or a con, depending on the person. Preserving food means you will get to spend more time in the kitchen if that is something you like. You will be able to prepare your food just the way you like.

In addition, food preservation simply gives people a major sense of accomplishment. All you have to do is stock up on the food items you want when they are cheap and abundant. Afterward, you can store and preserve them appropriately. That entire process should not take more than two or three hours if you are not fast. After that, you will have all the time you would have spent out grocery shopping to yourself, and you will feel like you have accomplished something great. I bet you did not know that you could feel so accomplished and relaxed from food!

Preserving food is also one way to teach you to be responsible. The chances are that most of you did not learn how to preserve and store food when you were younger. In addition, you will understand how much work goes into preserving food and learning new skills. You can pass on these skills to your children so they will not have to stumble on them as adults. Your children will also learn to work hard and be very responsible for their food when they have a home and a family of their own one day.

Finally, more importantly, food preservation can be fun! It can be fun to dehydrate, can, and freeze food! Your food can taste much better afterward, and you will feel much more satisfied and excited for the next time you can preserve a new food. Food preservation is fun and easy. I guarantee it will be more fun than dragging yourself off the grocery store or marketplace daily.

Food safety has become a concern for most people as food prices increase drastically. There are also shortages of specific foods that are very important for people and families. Food preservation is an answer to any concerns that might come out of that, and you will be rewarded with new feelings of accomplishment, responsibility, and relaxation.

Furthermore, you have control over your food preservation. Therefore, everything you cook can be prepared exactly how you like it!

Chapter 4:

What Canning Supplies do you Need? Where to Find Them

Tools And Utensils for Canning

We can discuss the proper canning equipment now that we are familiar with the overview of canning. There is a huge misconception that you need a lot of equipment to do this process, but that is not true. Your general investment can be anywhere from twenty-five dollars to a hundred and fifty dollars, including your pots, pans, jars, and other necessities.

You can find these prepping tools at Amazon, Targets, or any local hardware store. You might already possess most of these items in your arsenal of cooking ware. Once you make these purchases, you will likely never have to buy them again. Please make sure you read and follow this section carefully to avoid any unnecessary mistakes that could lead to a potentially dangerous situation.

Water Bath Canners

The water bath canner is a very large pot that normally has capacity size of 20 (or larger) quarts. It has a lid that seals pretty tight to keep the pressure and the temperature high within the can. This particular canner also comes equipped with a wooden or wire rack.

The purpose of the rack is to keep the boiling water equally distributed around the jars to ensure that all of the jars are processed. Because the rack makes it possible for the jars to have their own area within the pot, you don't have to worry about the jars contacting each other, which would increase the risk of the jars breaking while they are within the pot.

Don't Want to Buy a Water Canner

Suppose you are not interested in buying a fancy water canner or already have a large pot. In this case, instead of buying a water canner, you can save some money and use what you have or buy a large pot.

To skip buying a water canner, use any large metal pot deep enough to hold jars with an inch of boiling water on top. Now there is such a thing as having a pot that is too large. The standard pot for canning should not be four inches wider than your stove burner. If your pot is too large, some jars will not be processed as equally as the others.

The next step is replacing the rack; you still need something to act as a buffer to keep jars from bumping into each other and cracking inside the pot. You can secure the jars in place by either wrapping them in a clean dish towel or placing rings inside the pot. Either method will work.

Pressure Canners

A pressure canner is a large pot. The difference between this canner and the water canner is that the pressure canner is a stainless-steel heavy-duty pot made strong enough to endure extreme steam and pressure. The lid of this canner comes with a vent and a rubber seal to stop any air from seeping into the can, which may disrupt the process. A rack is also included with the pressure canner and serves the same purpose as the rack in the water canner.

One more thing to note is that there are two types of pressure canners. One comes with a dial, and the other comes with a weighted gauge. I think one is not better than the other as they provide the same result.

Jars

The jar is where you put the food that you want to process. There are three parts of a jar: the metal screw band, the metal lid, and the jar. Some types of jars that can be used for food include Mason jars and Ball jars. You could also use any type of threaded jar that comes with a self-sealing lid. These jars also have a wide opening, approximately three inches, so you can easily empty and fill them.

Jars can come in sizes ranging from ½ a pint up to ½ gallon. They can be reused numerous times until they wear out. You will know that a jar is worn out if it has any type of chip or fraction within the glass. If the jar is even slightly chipped, it will disrupt the seal and possibly break in the canner while you are canning your food.

Jar Lids

The lid is one of the most important parts when it comes to sealing the jar and keeping out the air. The jars sold in today's market come with a two-piece lid with a self-sealing compound that includes a metal disc and a ring.

Since the lid is small and thin and is easily softened when it is heated, it is a must that you dispose of the lid once you are done using it. However, you can reuse the metal screw bands/rings numerous times because they hold the lid in place while it's being processed.

Other Utensils To Use

Here is a quick reference to other utensils that you will use during your canning process.

- Jar lifter/ Tongs: Needed to lift the hot jars out of the boiling hot water.
- Funnel: For pouring the food into the jars and minimizing the mess
- Lid wand: It magnetically allows you to place the lid on or off the can.
- Clean cloths: Necessary for cleaning the rim of the jars and other messes
- Narrow, flat rubber spatula: Used to remove the air bubbles

Equipment Not to Use for Canning

- Pressure Cooker
- Dishwashers
- Microwave ovens

- Fruit Jars
- Mayonnaise Jars
- Metal Spatula

What Are the Right Jars?

Not all the jars are made for canning. When we talk about canning jars, they are available in various sizes and finishes. It all depends on what you are planning to can; here is the info to guide you in selecting the right jars.

Quart jars: You can use these jars for large foods, for example, whole tomatoes, or for a generous amount of food such as soup for many people or spaghetti sauce.   These jars are available in regular-mouth and wide-mouth styles.

Pint jars: This is the most versatile-size jar. The container can hold just about anything: veggies to serve one or two people, relishes, pickles, and smaller amounts of sauces. Pint jars are available in regular-mouth and wide-mouth styles.

Half-pint jars: These jars spot straight interior sides that allow you to get every last bit out of each jar. Some have a quilt or other designs on the exterior. Regular-mouth jars are taller than broad-mouth half-pint jars.

4-ounce jars: These are small jars for small portions of food or fruit. They are a great choice if you are making a big batch of jams for your family and friends.

Decorative jars: These glass jars are perfect for refrigerator-pickled foods that do not call for heat processing. Just ensure to clean them in hot, soapy water and rinse properly before filling them.

Vintage jars: are old canning jars with spring-type lids or colored glass.   Though they are pretty collector pieces, they should not be used in modern canning. They do not seal properly, may crack, and have uneven sizes. Do not use them for canning; rather, display them on a shelf.

Make sure you use only standard canning jars. They are made to resist the heat in a canner, and their mouths are especially threaded to be properly sealed with canning lids- you won't be happy to find your canned food spoiled soon after. Examine them carefully before using them and remove any chipped or cracked ones. To remove mineral deposits and hard-water film from empty jars, soak them in a solution consisting of 1 C. of vinegar to one gallon of water for a few hours. Purchase canning jars in grocery, discount, or hardware stores, or order them online.

Jars for Canning with a Wide Mouth: Using jars for canning with a wide mouth makes it easier to pack whole vegetables and fruits into a jar. They are suitable for foods like pickles since the broad mouth makes it easier to use your fingers or utensil to take out just a pickle at a time.

Regular-mouth canning jars: these are the pints and quart jars with shoulders. Wide-mouth half-pint jars are shorter than the regular-mouth ones. The later mouths are narrower than the former and are perfect for soups, sauces, or crushed vegetables and fruits.

Chapter 5:
Water-Bath Canning Step-By-Step Guide

Canning in a water bath is a procedure that requires placing the jar that is full of food into water that is boiling and steaming at the same time. After the water has been brought to a boil, the jar is placed in it and the two are allowed to continue boiling together for the allotted amount of time. This time restriction shifts around depending on the kind of food you're trying to keep preserved in your pantry.

The water bath canning needs to be done accurately following each step. You should use this method for processing foods like jams and pickles, which have high acidity. Endeavor to confirm how much time the food needs for processing as it is different for each recipe. Here are the steps to follow while canning the food using a roiling water bath.

Step 1: Preparation

There are certain initial preparations like sterilizing the lids and jars. However, it is unnecessary if you need to process the jar for more or less ten minutes.

After doing all the washing and sterilizing, prepare the water bath canner. It will help if you keep a stand-by kettle filled with boiling water for filling the canner quickly if required.

Bring the water up to a temperature of 140 degrees Fahrenheit by bringing it to a boil. For hot packing, the boiling temperature should be 180 F.

Step 2: Fill Food In The Jars

Always check the jars and lids for any imperfections like cracks. Use a perfect jar and new lids for canning with no chips or cracks. It would be best to give the jar a run in the dishwasher. Now, swiftly fill the canning jar using a ladle.

When the jar is filled, stir the food using a chopstick or spatula. This step ensures that there is no air bubble trapped inside the jar.

Step 3: Shut Off The Jars

All the jars have round lids specific for canning. You should place them accurately on the mouth of the jar and secure them with a lid wand. Keep screwing the bands unless the lids are airtight. Ensure that they are not too tight as the air needs to escape from the jar during processing.

Step 4: Processing The Jar

Take a jar lifter and start lifting the jars one by one. You should lower each jar into the water canner. This step requires care as the position of the jar should always be vertical in the water bath. When filling the jars, place them half an inch apart and fill them with water to within an inch of the jar's rim.

Turn up the heat and bring the water to a rolling boil. Close the saucepan with a cover and let the jars to process until the timer reaches the stated time.

Step 5: Cooling The Jars

You should start lifting the jars from the water vertically and put them outside on the shelf. The jars should be at a distance of one inch from each other. Always position cooling towels or a rack for putting the jar in. Let the jars cool for roughly 12 to 14 hrs before using them.

Step 6: Store The Jars

After the jars have cooled down, check whether they are shut tightly. Press down your finger on the lid to check the jar's seal. If they are not sealed properly, the jars will wiggle.

Now you should start removing the rings from the jars. If you can lift the jar from the lid, there is no need to worry about proper sealing. Now use a clean, damp towel to wipe the inside and outside of the jars. You need to find a spot that is cool and dark to store the jars.

Chapter 6:
The Importance of Home Canning

Benefits of Home Canning

It is becoming increasingly common to can food at home. This can be attributed to the rise in food costs, and individuals understand that they need to be more vigilant about safeguarding their food supply. Canning food at home is a perfect way to eat more locally grown produce. Canning is a perfect method to preserve the abundance of a specific crop during its peak season and keep it available throughout the year.

Whether you are a full-time canning enthusiast or just a hobbyist, you may approach home canning in various ways. Aside from saving money and helping the local economy, making your jam and jellies may be a fun weekend hobby or a serious way to boost your nutrition. As the global food market continues to deteriorate, you will likely save money. You will be able to reuse the jars that hold your home-canned goods, unlike the disposable packaging that comes with store-bought food.

How Preserving Food at Home Helps You:

When you utilize high-quality vegetables and follow the proper canning method, you will end up with a product that tastes better than anything you can buy at a supermarket. You can't purchase the quality of home-canned food, which is why so many recipes are tasty and worth the effort. You can make these delectable dishes in your kitchen.

Home canning gives you complete control over where your food comes from. If you can't grow your food, look for organic farms in your area or any other nearby farm that raises livestock. You'll be able to pick your food at its ripest from any of these options. By making your cans at home, you may also decrease your exposure to Bisphenol A, which is found in the cans of many mass-produced food goods. Humans are becoming increasingly aware of the dangers of bisphenol A, an endocrine disruptor.

As a consumer, you support the local economy by purchasing goods directly from local farmers. Since large commodities buyers don't determine pricing, local producers choose to sell from their farms or market stalls. The local economy benefits from this since small-scale farmers, especially those in rural areas, can maintain profitability.

It takes a lot of energy to manufacture and transport food consumed by society, which has a large carbon dioxide footprint. Highly industrialized agriculture also uses pesticides, herbicides, and petrochemical fertilizers. In the long run, this is detrimental to the ecosystem and reduces the soil's ability to produce food, resulting in rising food costs and shortages. A large portion of the transportation expenses connected with sending food across continents is eliminated when you buy local produce and can it at home. Preserving food at home does indeed demand some energy. Still, it pales compared to food that must be trucked across the nation to fill a supermarket shelf. Limiting the amount of far-flung food you consume minimizes the number of fossil fuels you use. Also, while purchasing local food, look for producers that utilize environmentally friendly techniques.

A feeling of satisfaction – The moment you start preserving food, you will be overjoyed. Because you did, you'll feel like you've accomplished something significant in your life! For much of human history, most people were preoccupied with ensuring that they had enough food to consume. I am not advocating a return to the days of foraging for food in the field. Still, I do believe that most people have a strong desire to be involved in obtaining and preparing their food. Fast food from a drive-through window in an SUV is not satisfying. Using a lot of energy to produce low-quality goods is a waste.

You need to learn the basics of home canning to get started in the kitchen and engage in food preservation. When you first start canning, it might be a little frightening, but after a few jobs, you will feel more confident in your abilities. Home canning raises certain safety concerns, but these may be addressed by following the instructions that come with each activity. To learn how to safely can food at home, check out the resources provided by Mason jar makers (which are a need), USDA, and several university agricultural departments. With a little research and practice, you will soon be able to put up delicious, locally grown food in your home canner.

Chapter 7:

Why Preserve Food?

The amount of food thrown out each year is beyond comprehension, despite the fact that we all know that food is essential to our survival. For example, India annually throws out 67 million tons of food worth around 92,000 crores. To put it another way, the sum is sufficient for the entire state of Bihar for a year. For any fast-developing or developed country, this is an issue that must be dealt with. Looking at the figures above, one would understand the economic importance of food preservation.

What Is the Purpose of Preserving Food?

Preserving food in the following methods can be quite beneficial:

1. Food preservation is about preventing food from going bad before it is eaten. Bacteria and other microbes can produce toxins that infect food or render it unsafe. Toxic and sometimes deadly cases of food poisoning are the end consequence.

2. The cost of home-preserved food is influenced by various factors. All materials, equipment, fresh food, human energy, and fuel energy are included in the cost of producing and storing food. When it comes to saving money, preserving fresh vegetables from the garden or farm is also a good idea. The utilization of locally grown and seasonal food, the reuse of preserving jars, and improved packing and food miles are all ecologically beneficial components of this method.

3. Agricultural excess is one of the primary causes for food preservation.

4. It also prevents agricultural planning that isn't proper.

Chapter 8:
How Does Canning Preserve Food?

The process of putting food in containers or canisters and then heating it to a specific temperature is known as canning. This allows for the food to be preserved for longer periods of time. Because microorganisms are killed by high heat and enzymes are deactivated, the diet's quality and reliability are both improved.

Canning is an important method for the preservation of food that may also be done in a safe manner if it is done properly. The process of canning is placing food products in containers and warming them to a temp that is high enough to kill bacteria that could result in illness or food going bad. Canning also has the effect of deactivating enzymes that might otherwise contribute to the spoilage of the food. During the process of heating, the air inside the jar is driven out, as well as a suction sealing is created once the jar has cooled. The vacuum sealing prohibits air from getting into the product, which in turn stops bacteria from spreading throughout the meal. Water-bath canning, often known as "boiling water bath canning," is a simpler way of preserving homemade jam, pickles, and tomato sauce. After the procedure, the food may retain its fresh taste for a year by processing the jars in hot water. Fruits, jams, juices, jellies, other fruit spreads, salsas, chutneys, the majority of tomatoes, pickles, relishes, sauces, spoonsful of vinegar, and condiments can all be safely preserved using the water bath canning method. Water bath canning is advised because these frequent foods contain substantial acid concentrations or the recipe contains the proper acid balance. The delectable high-acid menu has sweet and savory options.

However, preserving foods that are low in acidity can only be done securely through the process of pressure canning. Foods that are low in acidity include things like vegetables, meats, fish, and poultry. The required temperature of 240 degrees Fahrenheit or greater is achieved using pressurized steam, killing the natural bacterial spores in these foods. A vacuum is created inside the jars as they freeze, which maintains the food's freshness and stops any newly formed bacteria from tainting it. Canning low-acid vegetables and proteins requires a temperature of 240 degrees Fahrenheit and a pressure canner. Processing and canning of acidic foods, such as fruits, can be done in boiling hot water (ten pounds pressure at sea level). Tomatoes have an acidity level that is between low and high. They can be canned in boiling water, but you will need to add acid to boost the acidity.

Low-Acid Food Canning

A meal that is low in acidity has a pH that is greater than 4.6, while a meal that is high in acidity has a pH that is lower than 4.6, as can be seen in Figure 1 (below). This particular bacterium, Clostridium botulinum, is responsible for the production of a dormant form known as a spore. Because of this, the number is very important. Such microbes are hard to eradicate, and even if they do not germinate, they can survive dormant for years. Because Clostridium botulinum spores cannot live in the presence of oxygen, an incorrectly prepared meal potentially create an excellent habitat for them. The bacterium Clostridium botulinum produces a neurotoxin, which is considered to be one of the deadliest toxins ever found. This toxin, which can be present in extremely low concentrations, is responsible for botulism, an illness that is transmitted through food. If the meal has a pH of 4.6 or above, then Clostridium botulinum spores may form; otherwise, they will not. When low-acid meals with only a pH more than 4.6 are canned, these spores have to be heated to death in order for the canning process to be successful. Canned meals that are low in acid need to be pressure-cooked for extended periods of time at high temperatures in order to kill these spores, which are extremely resistant to heat. Temperatures of 240 degrees Fahrenheit (115.6 degrees Celsius) or more are typically used, and the processing times can range anywhere between twenty mins to many hours.

The bulk of vegetables, meat, and poultry fall into the category of low-acid foods. There are a lot of precise standards controlling the manufacturing of low-acid meals due to the requirement of ensuring correct processing.

Anyone who wants to can goods with a low acid content is required to register with the Food and Drug Administration (FDA), use only permitted equipment, attend a "Better Process Control School," and keep detailed records in accordance with official guidelines (21CFR Part 113 for FDA-regulated foods and 9 CFR Part 318 for USDA-regulated foods). The canning process is required to be inspected and certified by a Certified Process Authority as well. An Acknowledged Process Authority is an individual who is recognized as having the knowledge, experience, and equipment necessary to evaluate or verify the sufficiency of a thermal process. This can be done in order to ensure that the thermal process in question is adequate. This individual acts as a neutral source of information for both the processor and the regulatory bodies. Private firms, institutions, and trade groups may be linked with recognized process authorities.

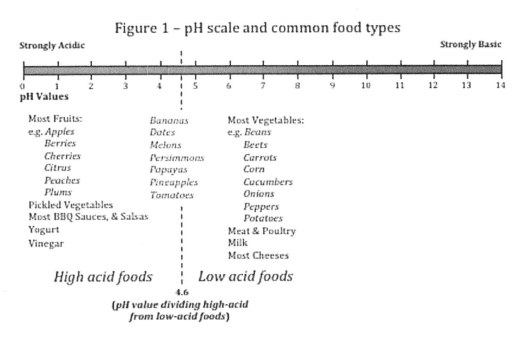

Figure 1 – pH scale and common food types

Foods With High Acidity

Examples of foods that are high in acid include jams and jellies, pickles, and the majority of fruits. On the other hand, they require less heating because there is no risk of Clostridium botulinum developing in them. In order for these foods to be consumed without risk, the required temperatures for pasteurization must be met. When pasteurizing foods with a pH of 3.5 or lower, temperatures of 175 degrees Fahrenheit (79.5 degrees Celsius) are sufficient. Pasteurization must be done at a temperature of 185 degrees Fahrenheit (85 degrees Celsius) for foods with a pH ranging from 3.5 to 4.0. For foods with a pH ranging from 4.0 to 4.3, the recommended temperature for pasteurization is 195 degrees Fahrenheit (90.5 degrees Celsius). Foods with a pH between 4.3 and 4.5 should be pasteurized at temperatures of 210 degrees Fahrenheit (99 degrees Celsius).

These temperatures used for pasteurization are sufficient to kill all microorganisms; the only exception to this rule is bacterial spores. Because of the food's acidic pH, it is considered to be commercially sterile, meaning that spores cannot grow on it and therefore it cannot spread disease. Because of this, a dish that is high in acid will not require the high-temperature remedy that a dish that is low in acid does. There is typically no need for pressure cooking when preparing a meal with a high acid content because the meal can be prepared at normal atmospheric stresses in heated water or in a steam bath. In this method of food preparation, the container is left sealed and placed in a water bath, where it is heated for two to ten minutes, depending on the food's pH level and other characteristics, till the internal temperature of something like the point of slowest heating reaches the required temperature for pasteurization. A Recognized Process Authority will ascertain the amount of time necessary to reach this temperature after analyzing the food, analyzing the process, and possibly performing heat penetration tests.

It is essential to not overcrowd the canisters in a water or steam bath procedure, as this will not allow for adequate room for the product to expand as it is being processed. Throughout the process, you must make sure that the containers are completely submerged in water in order to prevent under-processing and ensure that the heat penetration is consistent. A headspace of at least 14 inches (or 7 millimeters) is required to be present between the rim of the vessel as well as the top of the food or brine.

An alternative method of preparation involves bringing the high-acid food product to temperatures at which it can be pasteurized and then pouring it while it is still hot into jars before closing them. The terms "hot-filling" or "hot-fill/hold" are frequently used. The hot-filling method is successful when carried out appropriately. Keep in mind that the lid must be placed on the jar before the food's temperature can drop to the point where it can no longer be pasteurized. As a consequence of this, it is recommended that the meal be heated to a temperature that is 5 or 10 degrees higher than the temperature required for pasteurization prior to the filling. It allows you enough time to finish filling the container before you have to seal it. If the product's recommended temperature for pasteurization is 185 degrees Fahrenheit (85 degrees Celsius), for e.g., this should be boiled to around 195 degrees Fahrenheit (90.1 degrees Celsius) before being filled.

When employing a hot-fill approach, keep in mind that in order to kill any bacteria, the interior surfaces of the container, the jar neck, and the lid all need to reach temperatures high enough to be considered pasteurized. A prudent strategy for achieving this goal is to after filling and closing each container, turn it upside down and maintain this position for at least two minutes. It facilitates the sterilization of the inner jar surfaces by the hot product. If desired, the jars may be chilled after the hold time.

It is important to keep in mind that the hot-filling method might not work for large particle items such as whole pickled cucumbers or beets since the pieces need to be inserted into the jar first before being coated with hot brine. Although the saline is simmering, the amount of food items inside the container may cause the temperature of the filling brine to drop below the minimum required for safe pasteurization before the container can be sealed. Processing in a steam or hot water bath could be the only choice for many different things.

The glass jars used for the pasteurization process should be readied to temper the glass and prevent heavy food freezing during the hot filling process, no matter what heat processing method is employed. The temperature that should be used is 140 degrees Fahrenheit or 60 degrees Celsius.

In meals that are high in acid yet have not yet been fully cooked, the most common type of spoilage that can be detected is yeast or mold growth. The most common sign of mold deterioration is the presence of mold growth that may be seen on the top of the container (mold requires oxygen to grow). The degradation of yeast results in an increasingly cloudy liquid and, in certain instances, an expansion of the container. This is because fermentation results in the accumulation of gas pressure within a sealed container. Yeast and mold deterioration is evident in the food that has been accidentally consumed, although they often do not cause substantial sickness even if the item has been eaten. On the other hand, there have been instances in which the growth of yeast or mold has resulted in the natural acids in the food being consumed. As a consequence of this, the pH of the meal rises to the point where Clostridium botulinum has a chance to flourish and produce the toxin that causes botulism. As a direct consequence of this, the growth of yeast and mold in high-acid canned goods must be regarded as a potentially serious issue. Containers that have obvious or suspected spoilage should be thrown away, and this includes those that have a thin coating of mold on the surface.

Chapter 9:
Which Food Can be Canned and Which Can Not?

When choosing the best foods that can be used for canning, there are certain things to consider. Once you begin canning, you will figure out that you could "can" almost all types of foods. However, you have to be cautious about the techniques and their applications. While you might be tempted to store different kinds of meals or foodstuffs, it would be better for your health and safety that you avoid the tricky ones. Canning does preserve your food for months or even a year, but you have to be prepared to consume it within that period. Therefore, it is important to select the ingredients or cooked meals that you like or would help you survive in the long term. If you want to be smart and strategic about food preservation, you have to pick foods that work well with canning. Some foods can be canned quickly, while others might take an hour or two longer. Canning at home involves using two major methods to secure food items into jars and containers. These are pressure canning and water bath canning. Both processes are based on heating the foods; they are easy and simple.

With a water canner, you can just put the containers in water and boil them for a given amount of time so that the lid seals. You heat the foods in the jars for pressure canning through steam from a pressure cooker. This allows the elimination of bacteria and a highly toxic microorganism. Before making your food choices, you have to consider these techniques and then list the items. Some of the foods you select will be canned with the water bath procedure, while others require pressure. To pick out the best way, you have to get a clear idea of the fruits, meats, vegetables, or sauces that can be canned and preserved. Now, this involves a bit of scientific knowledge. You see, when organizing food items by their canning methods, you have to become familiar with their acidic nature or values. This can be slightly tricky and might have you wondering its importance.

Well, both the canning processes rely on the amount of acid found in a raw or pre-cooked item, so they have to be sorted out accordingly. The foods with low acidic value, more than 4.6 pH, have to be canned with pressure, whereas those with high acidic content can go through water bath canning. This brings us to the next question. What are the different items that belong to each of these groups? Generally, this is how you break it down.

Items that are low in acid

- All vegetables
- Meats
- Dairy and such products
- Seafood
- Poultry

Items that are high in acid

- Fruits including tomatoes
- Relishes and pickles

The food items listed above are everyday foods that can be preserved with canning. They ensure that you and your family are covered when things fall apart. In addition, you can also can sauces, chutneys, and fillings for pies through the water bath canning method, as they have a high acidic value. If you want to keep your condiments with you, you can add salsa and ketchup to this list too. For healthy prepared foods such as stock or broth, you will have to look towards pressure canning as it allows them to last longer and maintain their nutrition.

If you think about it, canning and preserving food is quite an interesting activity and one that you might enjoy. You can successfully build up your storage and stockpile for the future without being concerned with your food running out. Before you rush off to look through your pantry and buy a load of groceries to begin canning, you should be well-informed and equipped. Otherwise, you will find yourself stuck with a particular item and struggling to can it in the best way possible.

Experts have determined that pickling is an efficient way to can items that would otherwise be difficult. Because of this, it is essential to be aware that some of the ingredients might not be canned in their natural state in all cases. You will have to pickle them first or opt for freezing instead. It would be better to preserve broccoli, cauliflower, and cabbage in their pickled and processed form rather than chopping them up raw. Once this is done, it becomes easier to seal and lock the jars or containers by water bath canning, as that ideally works for pickled foods.

While canning your stock and preparing, try to avoid storing a lot of sweets or items with high-fat content. This is mainly because the heat affects them and makes them lose their appearance or taste. You don't want your meal to become mushy and deposit at the bottom of the container. In the end, the important factor is that the foods you choose must be easy to can and edible after a certain period. Desserts and munching candies might not be at the top of the list, but you can certainly include them somewhere. Other than that, some foods and ingredients are incredibly adaptive to canning and require minimal effort to go through the process. These are basically the best foods that you can opt to can quickly when preparing for emergencies.

Tomatoes

You really cannot survive without this absolutely essential item. All you have to do is peel and take out the additional elements from the core. Then you can just put them into jars and put in lemon juice so that the acidity levels rise. Cover with the lid and make sure it is tightly closed. Once this is done, you can introduce them to the heat in the water canning method and boil them for approximately forty to fifty minutes.

Beans

No matter your plans or where you want to go, beans should be one of the first foods you can. This efficient foodstuff can help you get through when there is a low food supply, and you cannot find anything else. Take the required quantity and seal them tightly in a container or jar. Since they are low in acids, the process you will carry out is pressure canning. It can take up to twenty to thirty minutes.

Cucumbers

There are different kinds of canned cucumbers that you find in a store. You might come across them in the form of dill or pickles, as the processing help them maintain their original form and crunchy texture. In canning, you can opt for slicing them before putting them into jars or get the smaller ones, which are easier to store in a container. They can then be canned through the water bath procedure in a short span of time. If you choose to pickle them, it should only take around five to ten minutes because you do not want to end up overcooking or making the contents soft.

Corn

With this, you can hardly go wrong. When canned, corn retains its freshness and taste throughout consumption. You have to boil it before putting it in a jar and canning it in a pressure canner. When you put the cover back on, don't forget to leave some headspace—at least an inch or two. While the overall time might be longer than almost all the other foods, it will be well worth it. In pressure canning corn, you may have to wait for an hour and thirty minutes to ensure that the containers are properly sealed and locked.

Fruits

Fruit canning is fairly easy and only takes about fifteen minutes. The steps required are also quite simple. You take the fresh fruit, wash it and keep it in a jar or container. Do not fill up to the top and save at least half to one inch of space. Then you can begin with water bath canning and have your fruits canned safely for eating later.

Fresh Greens

Now, you already know that vegetables are to be canned with pressure and it may take an hour or more to finish with everything. For leafy greens, you need to take fresh ones and then put them in separate jars. Before you start with the process, you do have the option of adding salt as well.

Once, you have picked out the foods you want to can and have stocked up on the necessary items, you can proceed towards the actual steps.

What Shouldn't I Pressure Can?

While pressure canning opens the doors to many recipe possibilities, there are still a handful of foods that are unsafe to preserve or don't taste good after pressure canning. . Here's my list of what not to pressure can:

Dense foods like mashed potatoes are not recommended because the heat cannot adequately penetrate the center, putting the food at risk for microorganism growth. It is recommended that potatoes, pumpkins, and squash be cubed and covered in water for canning. They may be mashed prior to using/eating.

● Milk and milk-based creams are not recommended for home canning because there hasn't been enough research by our states' extension programs to publish a "seal of approval." So why do we see evaporated and condensed milk sold in cans at the store?

–Milks (and creams) are commercially canned in aluminum. The pasteurization process heats milk to 275°F, exceeding what we can achieve in our home kitchen via pressure canning.

–Commercial canneries purposely and drastically reduce the temperature of the milk when canning to avoid it lingering in the temperature danger zone of 60°F to 90°F, preventing the growth of pathogenic microorganisms. This is also something we cannot achieve in our home kitchen because our containment source is a glass jar. Glass cannot handle a vast swing in temperature without breaking, fracturing, or shattering.

● Delicate, soft-skinned fruits and berries, such as strawberries, turn brown and become mushy in a pressure canner. Exposure to high temperatures is often too much for a delicate berry; therefore, the food's integrity breaks down, becoming mushy and brown. These color and texture changes don't make the foods inedible, but they are certainly unappealing.

Chapter 10:

Canning Safely

The goal of preserving food, regardless of the approach taken, is to maintain the food in a usable state so that it can be consumed at a later time. Infections caused by bacteria, fungi, or parasites can result in a wide range of symptoms, from diarrhea to death. These diseases, in addition to the factors that cause them, should not be treated lightly. The CDC estimates that around 48 million people in the United States become ill each year as a result of a disease that is spread by contaminated food. One hundred twenty-eight thousand of them are admitted to hospitals, and 3,000 of them die. According to the most recent CDC data, Norovirus, Salmonella, and Campylobacter were the most prevalent causes of sickness in 2011. Why do illnesses and diseases that are caused by food become prevalent, then why are there far too many of them nowadays? These are permissible questions to ask if you are in a reasonable state and surrounded by reasonable individuals. The answers are both easy and challenging to implement.

Did you know that TB, typhoid fever, and cholera were common food-borne illnesses in the last few decades of the 19th century? In today's youngsters, an illness known as Hemolytic Uremic Syndrome (a form of acute kidney failure) is caused by E. coli O157:H7. We also know that infection with Campylobacter can cause Guillain-Barre Syndrome, which is a form of autoimmune disorder marked by a weakening in the muscles.

Infectious pathogens may now spread more swiftly than in the past due to easier movement. In addition, these microbes continue to evolve over time, which can result in changes to their characteristics as well as the indications of the illnesses that they inflict.

Whether or not a bacterium makes its way into our food supply is determined by a number of factors, including unsafe manufacturing procedures, environmental impacts, ecology factors, production practices, and consumption patterns.

Lab tests are also being improved, which enables the detection of a far greater number of infectious agents than was ever before possible. In addition, the importance of simultaneous worldwide communication is not something that should be disregarded.

The most important thing you can do to protect yourself and your loved ones from being ill, even how unsettling it may be to learn this information, is to use your common sense. When it comes to the safety of food, the majority of cases of foodborne disease can be avoided if you take the following precautions:

- Be sure to give your hands a thorough washing before working with food, and check that all of the implements and working surfaces you use are equally clean.
- Ensure that the produce is thoroughly rinsed by holding it under running water and massaging the surface area using clean hands. It is not required to use soaps or detergents since the friction caused by the hands will release the dirt and grime that is retaining the bacteria, and running water will wash it away.
- Ensure that the product does not become soaked. When rinsing smaller goods, use colanders or sieves and be sure to keep the layers shallow. This will ensure that each berry, bean, or other food is washed as fully as possible on all of its surfaces.
- Never, under any circumstances, let liquid from raw meats come into contact with just about any gear or instrument which might come into contact with fruits and vegetables, or with the fruits and vegetables themselves. This includes even the tiniest of splatters.
- Sanitize everything that has come into contact with raw meat or the juices of raw meat.
- Always follow proper sanitation procedures when preserving any type of food product.
- If the use of sterilized equipment or containers is required, you must ensure that they are properly sterilized. Ensure that foods that are raw, cooked, processed, and unprocessed are always stored in different areas.

It is possible that the further steps will require a great deal of effort, in addition to much more time and effort. However, when compared to the amount of time necessary to recover from a foodborne disease, not to mention the amount of money that will likely be spent on hospitalization and medication, they are, at best, a minor irritation.

Food preservation is the process of removing germs from food or limiting their reproduction to unsafe levels. This can be accomplished by freezing, sugaring, salting, or canning the food.

Food that has been refrigerated or frozen is preserved in a condition of suspended animation, preventing germs from developing. At least two bacteria can thrive at refrigerator temperatures, which is unfortunate. Bacteria are also inhibited by high quantities of salt, sugar, or acid. Heat destroys most germs and pathogenic microbes. To eliminate pathogens like bacteria, viruses, and parasites, you only need to maintain a temperature of 78 degrees Celsius (160 degrees Fahrenheit) for a few seconds. Clostridium bacteria, on the other hand, are able to create a spore that is resistant to heat and can only be eliminated at temperatures greater than boiling. The pressure canning process generates the warmth necessary to eliminate these spores from the environment.

Heat does not alter all of the poisons generated by bacteria. As a consequence of this, it is essential to only preserve foods that are of good quality. Avoid:

- Bruised fruit
- Split peels or skins
- Evidence of insect attacks
- Nibbles by birds or animals

When storing products for future use, food safety should always come first. Make sure that everything is as fresh as it can possibly be and that it is prepared in proportions that are manageable and in little quantities as early as it is practicable. The greatest quality preserved foods are processed on the same day as they are collected and handled hygienically.

Chapter 11:

Tips and Tricks

Pressure Canning Safety Tips

Like all other culinary activities, pressure canning is accompanied by different risks. Hence, you need to take some precautionary measures to help you process your foods safely and appropriately. Below are some of the safety tips.

- Use the right and appropriate pressure canner in terms of size and quality.
- Use only jars that are in good shape.
- Always confirm the functionality of the gauge.
- Ensure that your pressure canner's gasket is soft and pliable always.
- Sanitation is important. Do not use any equipment except it is clean.
- Use endorsed recipes only.
- Do not over-heat or under-heat the canner.
- Stick to the processing time.
- Always allow your jars to cool naturally.

Jar Sterilization

Jar sterilization is a crucial stage that should not be overlooked. Water bath canning may seem like a straightforward process. However, some risks are associated with the procedure. Therefore, failure to follow the precautionary measures exposes the food to pollution, which may negatively affect health.

Sterilizing your jars is one of the steps that must be taken to safeguard the food you're preserving. According to some, jar sterilization is only necessary if you reside in a high-altitude location. Sterilizing your jars is recommended regardless of where you reside; the additional effort will not harm you.

Foods that need less than 10 minutes of processing must be placed in sterilized jars. Each recipe has a different processing time, so make sure you read the instructions well.

To properly sterilize the jars, please follow these steps:

1. Position your jars upside down on the side of the canning rack. The rack needs to be placed within the canner that uses a water bath.
2. Pour boiling water into the water bath plastic bucket as well as the containers until the rims of the containers are one inch higher than the water level. The water should be warm, not hot.
3. Boil the water for 10 to 15 minutes after bringing it to a boil.
4. To drain the sterilized jars, use jar lifters or tongs to remove them one at a time. Remember that the jars can get very hot. Don't rely solely on your hands to deal with them.
5. Replace the water in the canner by draining it and refilling it with fresh water.

After you have sterilized your jars, you may proceed with the remainder of the scanning procedure.

The lids and seals do not need to be sterilized in hot water. Hot water and detergent can be used to clean these. To ensure that you get rid of all of the soap, give them a thorough wash. Detergent residue may cause off-tastes in food, which is why cleaning your jars isn't the greatest technique to sterilize them.

When you reuse your jars, sterilizing them is also a good idea. Keep in mind that only the glass jars may be reused, not the lids or seals.

Jars, Lids and Seals

When you buy canning jars you must keep in mind that:

- You must use glass jars because they are the most appropriate for this type of method. People believe that the best ones are the mason-type jar. Never use mayonnaise jars because they are not appropriate.
- Make sure that your jars are not damaged or chipped because they may break during the boiling process. Even if they are damaged, but they have not broken during the boiling process, sealing will be inappropriate and the food inside the jars will rot.
- You can reuse the jars only if they are undamaged. Never forget to sterilize them again.
- Today there are jars of different sizes on the market, so choose the one that you like the most.

Every jar has a lid composed of a flat dish that allows you to seal the jar. It also has a metal screw used as a lid for the jar. You must change the lids after every procedure, particularly if they are flawed or dented. Even if experts believe lids can be replaced after five years of use. Read carefully the instructions provided by the jar manufacturers to obtain efficient canning.

Do's And Don'ts

Canning is simple, but you have to follow our instructions carefully because it can result in disastrous consequences.

- Never eat food if you suspect that it has gone bad. Just throw it away. Home-canned food can rot for several reasons. They include a crack in a jar, insufficient cooking time, and a dent in the lid. If you ever notice any of these signs, never taste them.
- Never put fat or butter into your home-canned products because they slow heat transfer during the boiling process and it will decrease food's life.
- Never add more spices than required by the recipe because it could be unsafe.
- Read carefully all the recipes because you have to know what to do and be organized.
- Never use overripe food for canning.

Temperature And Time of Processing

It is vital to utilize the correct processing parameters (temperature and time) when canning foods to ensure that the final product is safe to eat. If food is not properly processed, it will degrade. The amount of time it takes to complete a task depends on a variety of factors. The following are some of the components:

- The size and shape of the jars; less time is necessary for smaller jars.
- Whether they were cooked or uncooked when they were packed.
- The liquid volume in each jar; the contents of the jar might heat up quicker with more liquid.
- The quantity of food that is processed; smaller components will heat up faster.
- The canning procedure was applied.
- The adaptability of your location; at the very bottom of each chart, you'll find instructions for adjusting the processing time based on your location's elevation above sea level.

The preserving technique and the amount of time that the processing takes are both affected by all of these factors. Make every effort to follow the canning instructions properly. You'll need to adjust your processing timings as you climb higher. The temperature at which water boils at sea level is 212 degrees Fahrenheit; but, when altitude rises, the temperature at which water boils drops. At higher altitudes, the temps during which water boils do not reach high enough levels to effectively kill bacteria. It is necessary to extend the amount of time spent processing food in a boiling water bath in order to make up for low boiling temperatures. The graphs below demonstrate processing data and the changes in processing time that must be made for higher altitudes.

Water Bath Canning Time Table

Food Type	Pack Method	Process Time – Minutes	
		Pint Jars	Quart Jars
Apples	Hot	20	20
Apricots	Raw	25	30
	Hot	20	25
Blackberries	Raw	15	20
	Hot	15	15
Blueberries	Raw	15	20
	Hot	15	15
Cranberries	Hot	15	15
Cherries	Raw	25	30
	Hot	15	20
Cucumbers (pickled in vinegar brine)	Raw	10	15
Grapefruit	Raw	10	10
Grapes	Raw	15	20
	Hot	10	10
Nectarines	Raw	25	30
	Hot	20	25

Oranges	Raw	10	10
Peaches	Raw	25	30
	Hot	20	25
Pears	Raw	25	30
	Hot	20	25
Plums	Raw	20	20
	Hot	25	25
Raspberries	Raw	15	20
	Hot	15	15
Rhubarb	Hot	15	15
Strawberry Jam	Hot	5	-
Pineapple	Hot	15	20
Tomatoes – Halved or Whole - No Liquid Added (with acid added)	Raw	85	85
Tomatoes - Crushed (Quartered) - No Liquid Added (with acid added)	Hot	35	45
Tomatoes - Juice (with acid added)	Hot	35	40

Heat Processing Altitude Adjustments

Water will boil at a temperature of 212 degrees Fahrenheit when it is at sea level. As elevation increases, the temperature at which water boils decreases, which means that it is less effective at destroying pathogens. In order to make up for something like the low boiling point that occurs at higher altitudes, the processing times that take place in water baths need to be lengthened. When pressure canning at elevations exceeding 2,000 feet, the pounds of pressure utilized for safe processing must also be increased.

Altitude Feet	Increase processing time by:
1,001 – 3,000	5 minutes
3,001 – 6,000	10 minutes
6,001 – 8,000	15 minutes

8,001 – 10,000	20 minutes

Altitude Feet	Weighted gauge	Dial Gauge
0 – 1,000	10	11
1,001 – 2,000	15	11
2,001 – 4,000	15	12
4,001 – 6,000	15	13
6,001 – 8,000	15	14
8,001 – 10,000	15	15

The processing timeframes included within the instructions are dependent on either an altitude of two thousand feet or less for canning using pressure and an elevation of one thousand feet or less for canning using a water bath. Adjust your processing time as needed if you reside at a higher elevation.

Chapter 12: **Fruits**

1. Canned Oranges

Preparation time: 10 minutes   **Cooking time:** 15 minutes   **Servings:** 6

Ingredients:

- 3 oranges, peeled, removed white pith & divided into segments
- 5 whole cloves
- 1 cup sugar
- 2 cups water
- ½ tsp cinnamon

Directions:

1. In a saucepan, combine the sugar and the water. Mix in some cinnamon to taste. Bring the liquid to a boil.

2. Turn the heat down and keep it at a simmer for five minutes.

3. Pack orange segments into the clean jars and top with cloves.

4. Pour sugar syrup over the orange while it is still hot. Ensure that there is a 1/16-inch headspace. Remove the air bubbles.

5. Process the jars in a warm water bath for ten minutes, then remove the lids.

6. Let the jars cool completely in the water bath.

7. Check seals of jars. Label and store it

Per serving: Calories: 169Kcal; Fat: 0.1g; Carbohydrates: 44.3g; Protein: 0.9g

2. Canned Pineapple

Preparation time: 10 minutes **Cooking time:** 60 minutes **Servings:** 24

Ingredients:

- 6 large pineapples, peeled, cored & cut into chunks
- 5 cups of water
- 1 cup sugar

Directions:

1. Put the sugar and water in the pot, bring it up to a boil, and stir it frequently while it's cooking until the sugar is completely dissolved. Turn the heat down to low.

2. Add pineapples chunks and cook for 10 minutes.

3. Pack pineapple chunks into the clean jars. Leave ½-inch headspace.

4. The warm sugar syrup should be poured over the pineapple chunks. Keep a headspace of a quarter of an inch. Get rid of any air bubbles.

5. Jars should have their lids on before being processed for ten minutes in a water bath that is boiling.

6. Take the jars out of the water bath and allow them to cool down to room temperature.

7. Check seals of jars. Label and store it.

Per serving: Calories: 72Kcal; Fat: 0.1g; Carbohydrates: 19.2g; Protein: 0.4g

3. Canned Strawberries

Preparation time: 10 minutes   **Cooking time:** 20 minutes **Servings:** 4

Ingredients:

- 4 cups strawberries, washed & hulled
- ¼ tsp citric acid
- ½ cup sugar

Directions:

1. Place the sliced strawberries and sugar inside a large saucepan, cover, and allow it to remain at room temperature for six hours.

2. After adding the citric acid, set the pot over medium heat and continue to simmer for one minute, or until the strawberries have reached the desired temperature.

3. Take the pot off the burner. Place the strawberries in the jars that have been thoroughly cleaned, and then cover them with strawberry juice. Keep a headspace of half an inch. Get rid of any air bubbles.

4. Jars should have their lids on before being processed for ten minutes in a water bath that is boiling.

5. Take the jars out of the water bath and allow them to cool down to room temperature.

6. Check seals of jars. Label and store it.

Per serving: Calories: 140Kcal; Fat: 0.4g; Carbohydrates: 36.1g; Protein: 1g

4. Canned Peaches

Preparation time: 10 minutes   **Cooking time:** 30 minutes   **Servings:** 8

Ingredients:

- 4 lbs. peaches
- 8 cups water
- 1 ½ cups sugar

Directions:

1. Cook the peaches for three minutes in the water that has been brought to a boil.

2. Take the peaches out of the water that is boiling and drop them in the dish of icy water.

3. Peel peaches, discard the pit, and cut them into slices.

4. Pack peaches into the clean jars. Leave ¼-inch headspace.

5. Put the sugar and water in a pot, bring it to a boil, and stir it constantly until the sugar is completely dissolved.

6. Heated sugar syrup should be poured over the pears. Keep a headspace of a quarter of an inch. Get rid of any air bubbles.

7. Jars should have their lids on before being processed for twenty minutes in a water bath that is boiling.

8. Take the jars out of the water bath and allow them to cool down to room temperature.

9. Check seals of jars. Label and store it.

Per serving: Calories: 170Kcal; Fat: 0.2g; Carbohydrates: 44.5g; Protein: 0.7g

5. Canned Blueberries

Preparation time: 10 minutes **Cooking time:** 20 minutes **Servings:** 4

Ingredients:

- 3 lbs. blueberries, rinsed
- 1 cup sugar

- 4 cups Water

Directions:

1. Put the sugar and water in the saucepan, bring it up to a boil, and stir it constantly until the sugar is completely dissolved.

2. Pack blueberries in clean jars then pour hot sugar syrup over blueberries. Leave ½-inch headspace.

3. Jars should have their lids on before being processed for twenty minutes in a water bath that is boiling.

4. Take the jars out of the water bath and allow them to cool down to room temperature.

5. Check seals of jars. Label and store.

Per serving: Calories: 382Kcal; Fat: 1.2g; Carbohydrates: 99.3g; Protein: 2.6g

Chapter 13:

Fruit Juices

1. Strawberry and Blackberry Marmalade

Preparation time: 15 minutes **Cooking time:** 5 minutes **Servings:** 4-pint jars

Ingredients:

- 1 lemon
- 1 3/4 cups fresh strawberries, hulled and crushed
- 1 cup fresh blackberries, crushed
- 1 1/2 teaspoons freshly squeezed lemon juice
- 3 tablespoons powdered pectin
- 3 1/2 cups sugar

Directions:

1. Get ready to soak in some warm water. Put the jars in there so they can stay heated. After washing them in hot, soapy water, the rings and lids can be placed aside to dry.

2. Thoroughly wash the lemon in warm water with some dish soap. Remove as much of the pith (the lemon's white inner membrane) as you can by cutting away half of the rind off the lemon with a knife that is very sharp. After slicing the rind into small slices, cut each strip into pieces that are about a quarter of an inch long.

3. Mix the lemon rind with just enough water to cover it in a small saucepot and bring it to a boil over high heat. Bring the liquid to a boil. After straining, set aside the rind.

4. Mix the blackberries, strawberries, lemon peel, and lemon juice together in a saucepot of medium size that is put over high heat. In a slow, steady stream, mix in the pectin. Bring the blender to a full boil, stirring often.

5. Bring in the sugar. Bring the mixture back up to a full, rolling boil over high heat where it was originally cooked. When it becomes impossible to reduce the jam by stirring, set a timer for one minute and stir it continuously. Remove the pot from the heat.

6. With the heat off, stir the marmalade for 1 minute more to ensure even distribution of the rind before filling the jars. Skim off any foam.

7. Place the marmalade in the jars that have been prepared, leaving a headspace of about a quarter of an inch. Make use of a tool that does not contain any metal in order to pop any air bubbles. Remove any debris from the rims, then use the lids and rings to create a seal.

8. Place the jars in a pot filled with hot water and let them sit there for ten minutes. Turn off the heat and give the jars 10 minutes to cool down in the water bath before removing them.

9. Remove the jars from the canner that contains hot water as carefully as possible. Put to the side for a full day.

10. Make sure the lids have good seals on them. Remove the rings, clean the jars, label them with the date and name, and then store them in a cabinet or a pantry. Fridge them and use them within 3 weeks. Properly secure jars will last in the cupboard for 12 months.

Per serving: Calories: 49Kcal; Fat: 0.2g; Carbohydrates: 8.7g; Protein: 3.6g

2. Grapefruit Marmalade with Vanilla

Preparation time: 25 minutes   **Cooking time:** 60 minutes   **Servings:** 4-pint jars

Ingredients:

- 3 grapefruits
- 3 cups sugar

- 1 whole vanilla bean

Directions:

1. Prepare a hot water bath. Set the jars in it to keep warm. After washing them in warm, soapy water, the rings and lids can be placed aside to dry.

2. Wash the grapefruits well with warm, soapy water. With a sharp knife, remove the grapefruit rind. Stack into piles and slice into strips. Mince the strips.

3. Combine the chopped rind with just enough water to fill it in a small saucepan and heat it over medium heat. Raise the heat to a low simmer. Boil for twenty mins, or till crisp.

4. While the rind cooks, remove any remaining pith from the grapefruit with your hands or a knife. Working on a bowl to catch the juice, slice along the membranes, removing each grapefruit segment individually. attach the segments to the bowl with the juice. When finished, squeeze the remaining membranes over the bowl to collect any additional juice. Discard the membranes and seeds.

5. After straining the rind, set aside two cups of the cooking liquid for later use.

6. Combine the grapefruit segments together with their juices, sugar, and rind in a saucepot of medium size that is set over medium-high heat. You will need to conserve some of the cooking liquid for this step. Bring to a high boil with constant stirring. Cook for thirty-five to forty-five mins, or until a candy thermometer registers 220 degrees Fahrenheit (104 degrees Celsius), whichever comes first.

7. Mix in the seeds from the vanilla bean. Remove the pot from the heat. To determine whether or not the marmalade has been set, use the plate test. If not, place the pot back on the heat and continue to simmer it for increments of 5 minutes until the consistency is to your desire.

8. With the heat off, stir the marmalade for 1 minute to evenly distribute the rind. Skim off any foam.

9. Place the marmalade in the jars that have been prepared, leaving a headspace of about a quarter of an inch. Make use of a tool that does not contain any metal in order to pop any air bubbles. After cleaning the rims with a damp cloth, put on the lids and rings to create a seal.

10. Place the jars in a container with boiling water and let them sit there for ten minutes. Turn off the stove and let the jars sit in the water bath for ten minutes until the heat is turned off.

11. Remove the jars from the canner that contains hot water as carefully as possible. Placed to the side to chill for a period of 12 hours.

12. Make sure the lids have good seals on them. Remove the rings, thoroughly clean the jars, label them with the current date, and then store them in a closet or a pantry.

13. Use within 3 weeks.

Per serving: Calories 149Kcal; Fat: 0.4 g; Carbohydrates: 37.7 g; Protein 1.3 g

3. Blueberry Orange Marmalade

Preparation time: 15 minutes **Cooking time:** 25 minutes **Servings:** 3-pint jars

Ingredients:

- 1/2 cup water
- 1/8 teaspoon baking soda
- 1 small orange, peeled and chopped
- 1 small lemon, peeled and chopped
- 2 cups blueberries, crushed
- 2 1/2 cups sugar
- 1/2 (6-ounce) package liquid fruit pectin

Directions:

1. In a saucepan or cooking pot, merge the water and baking soda.

2. Bring the mixture to a boil, then continue cooking it for about ten minutes on low heat. Continuous stirring is necessary to avoid burning the food.

3. Put the sugar, berries, lemon, and orange in a bowl and mix them together.

4. Bring the mixture to a boil, then continue to simmer it for around five mins over medium heat. Continuous stirring is necessary to avoid burning the food.

5. Pectin should be incorporated, and the mixture should be allowed to simmer for about a minute over medium-low heat in order to become solid and thick. Continuous stirring is necessary to avoid burning the food.

6. Pour the heated mixture into the jars that have been previously sterilized, either directly or using a jar funnel. Maintain a headspace that is a quarter of an inch from the top of the jar.

7. Insert a spatula that is not made of metal and swirl the mixture gently to break up any teeny-tiny air bubbles that may be present.

8. Wipe the edges of the seal with a moist cloth to clean them. Put the lids on the jars, and then adjust the bands or rings so that the jars are completely sealed and nothing can leak out.

9. Place the jars in a container with boiling water and let them sit there for ten minutes.

10. Place the jars in an area that is cool, dry, and dark. Give them the chance to completely calm off.

11. Store in your refrigerator and use within 10 days.

Per serving: Calories 393Kcal; Fat: 0.1 g; Carbohydrates: 104.1g; Protein: 0.4g

4. Orange Marmalade

Preparation time: 15 minutes **Cooking time:** 15 minutes **Servings:** 2-pint jars

Ingredients:

- 1/2 cup water
- 4 medium navel oranges, peeled and cut into small pieces
- 2 cups sugar

Directions:

1. Put the orange pieces in a food processor or a blender to chop them up. Blend well.

2. Put the orange mixture, water, and sugar into a deep saucepan and stir to incorporate.

3. The mixture should be cooked for around 12–15 minutes over medium heat until it is firm and thick. The temperature should be set at 220 degrees Fahrenheit. Continuous stirring is necessary to avoid burning the food.

4. Pour the heated mixture into the jars that have been previously sterilized, either directly or using a jar funnel. Maintain a headspace that is a quarter of an inch from the top of the jar.

5. Insert a spatula that is not made of metal and swirl the mixture gently to break up any teeny-tiny air bubbles that may be present.

6. Wipe the edges of the seal with a moist cloth to clean them. Put the lids on the jars, and then adjust the bands or rings so that the jars are completely sealed and nothing can leak out.

7. Place the jars in an area that is cool, dry, and dark. Give them the chance to completely calm off.

8. Store in your refrigerator and use within 10 days.

Per serving: Calories: 17 Kcal; Fat: 0 g; Carbohydrates: 1g; Protein: 1g

Chapter 14:

Jams

1. Peach Spice Jam

Preparation time: 5 minutes **Cooking time:** 15-25 minutes **Servings:** 2-pint jars

Ingredients:

- 8-9 large peaches, pitted
- 3 cups sugar
- Juice and rind of 1/2 lemon
- 1/4 teaspoon allspice (optional)
- 1/4 teaspoon cloves (optional)

Directions:

1. Detach pits and imperfect parts from peaches.

2. Peaches should be given a quick parboil in a large pot with enough water to prevent them from catching fire. After the peaches have had enough time to become pliable, pour them thru a food mill.

3. Put the peaches and an amount of water that is sufficient to cover them in a large, profound pan or cooking pot. Boil until softened. Drain water.

4. Move the contents of the bowl to a mixer or food processor. Purée the mixture by blending it thoroughly.

5. To the cooking vessel, such as a pot or skillet, add the puree together with the other ingredients.

6. Bring the mixture to a boil and continue cooking it over medium-low heat till it reaches the desired consistency of being thick and solid. Always make sure to stir everything up to prevent burning.

7. Pour the heated mixture into the jars that have been previously sterilized, either directly or using a jar funnel. Maintain a headspace that is a quarter of an inch from the top of the jar.

8. Place a spatula that is not made of metal in the middle of the liquid and gently stir it around to break up any teeny tiny air bubbles.

9. Cleanse the borders of the seal. Put the lids on the jars, and then adjust the bands or rings so that the jars are completely sealed and nothing can leak out.

10. Place the jars in an area that is cool, dry, and dark. Give them the chance to completely calm off.

11. Store in your refrigerator for later use.

Per serving: Calories: 435Kcal; Fat: 1.4g; Carbohydrates: 11.4g; Protein: 5.1g

2. Blackberry Jam

Preparation time: 15 minutes **Cooking time:** 30 minutes **Servings:** 10-pint jars

Ingredients:

- 5 cups blackberries
- 2 cups sugar
- 2 tablespoons lemon juice

Directions:

1. Canners that use water baths are ideal for sterilizing bottles. Give the bottles some time to chill.

2. Put all of the ingredients in a pot on the stove. Bring to a boil and cook for ten minutes while stirring continuously. Turn the heat down to a simmer and wait until the sauce has thickened completely.

3. Take the pan off the heat and let it cool down a little bit.

4. After emptying the bottles of any air bubbles, carefully transfer to the clean containers. Put the cover back on.

5. Place in a canner that has a water bath and let it process for ten minutes.

6. Consume within a year.

Per serving: Calories: 196Kcal; Fat: 0.2g; Carbohydrates: 49.7g; Protein: 1.7g

3. Honeyberry Jam

Preparation time: 15 minutes **Cooking time:** 25 minutes **Servings:** 6 half-pint jars

Ingredients:

- 2 cups honeyberry fruit
- 2 cups sugar

Directions:

1. Utilize a water bath canner to sterilize the bottles. Let the bottles cool down.

2. All components should be put in a pot. Use a ladle or a potato masher to macerate the berries.

3. Set the temperature to medium-high and stir continuously as you bring the mixture to a boil. Once the heat is reduced to medium-low, let the mixture simmer for an additional 15 minutes, or until it thickens.

4. Turn the heat down and give the mixture a brief moment to cool.

5. Remove the air bubbles before transferring the mixture to sterilized bottles. Put the lid on.

6. Bring in the canner and process it for ten minutes.

7. Consume within a year.

Per serving: Calories: 190Kcal; Fat: 0.01g; Carbohydrates: 48.9g; Protein: 0.3g

4. Blueberry Vanilla Jam

Preparation time: 15 minutes **Cooking time:** 22 minutes **Servings:** 22 half-pint jars

Ingredients:

- 6 large canning bottles
- 1 1/4 pounds blueberries, rinsed and stems removed
- 3/4 cup granulated sugar
- 2 tablespoons lemon juice
- 1/2 vanilla bean pod, seeds scraped
- 1 teaspoon pectin

Directions:

1. Canners that use water baths are ideal for sterilizing bottles. Give the bottles some time to chill.

2. Put all of the ingredients in a pot, besides the pectin, and mash them together when the blueberries are completely broken down.

3. Place over high heat, and while stirring often, bring to a boil. Continue doing this for ten minutes. After you have removed the pod from the vanilla bean, whisk in the pectin. Keep stirring for another two minutes, or until the mixture reaches the desired consistency.

4. Pour the mixture into the sterile jars, making sure to leave a headspace of about a quarter of an inch. Take out the air bubbles, and then put the lid on with the screw.

5. Place in a manner that uses a water bath and proceed according to the normal canning guidelines for using a water bath.

6. Process for 10 minutes.

7. Consume within a year and keep refrigerated once the bottles are opened.

Per serving: Calories: 38Kcal; Fat: 0.2g; Carbohydrates: 9.2g; Protein: 0.19g

5. Mandarin Orange Jam

Preparation time: 15 minutes **Cooking time:** 22 minutes **Servings:** 5-pint jars

Ingredients:

- 5 bottling jars with a lid
- 2 pounds of mandarin oranges, peeled and seeded (about 10 to 12 oranges)
- Juice from 1 lemon, freshly squeezed
- 1 cup sugar

Directions:

1. Sterilize the bottles in a water bath canner.

2. Prepare the mandarin oranges by roughly chopping them. Put everything in the pot, except the pectin, and bring it up to temperature over a medium flame. In order to prevent the food from catching fire on the bottom, stir continuously for ten minutes.

3. After mixing in the pectin, continue stirring for a further two minutes.

4. Turn off the stove and let the temperature drop.

5. After transferring the orange jam inside the sterile bottles, check to see that there is at least a quarter of an inch of headspace left. Take care to eliminate the air bubbles. Put the cover back on.

6. Put the bottles in the canner that uses water bath processing. Perform the operation for ten minutes.

7. Use up within the next year.

Per serving: Calories: 169Kcal; Fat: 0.2g; Carbohydrates: 41.6g; Protein: 1.3g

Chapter 15:
Jellies and Other Fruit Spreads

1. Cherry Rhubarb Jelly

Preparation time: 10 minutes **Cooking time:** 30 minutes **Servings:** 32 Servings

Ingredients:

- 6 cups diced rhubarb
- 4 cups white sugar
- 6 ounces cherry gelatin
- 21 ounces cherry pie filling

Directions:

1. Refrigerate rhubarb, covered, overnight, after adding it to a bowl and pouring sugar over it.

2. Cook the rhubarb mixture over medium heat in a pot. After 30 minutes of stirring, turn off the heat and let it cool. Add the gelatin and the cherry pie filling and combine well. Let it cool and then pack it into jars. Store in the fridge or freezer.

Per serving: Calories: 164Kcal; Fat: 0g; Carbohydrates: 42.1g; Protein: 0.6g

2. Lemon & Wine Jelly

Preparation time: 10 minutes **Cooking time:** 30 minutes **Servings:** 40 Servings

Ingredients:

- ½ cup fresh lemon juice
- 3 ½ cups of wine
- 4 ½ cups white sugar
- 2 ounces dry pectin

Directions:

1. Pectin, lemon juice, and wine should all be combined in a single saucepan and then brought to a low boil.

2. After stirring in the sugar, continue cooking for approximately two minutes.

3. Remove the foam, then ladle the liquid into sterile containers.

4. After sealing the bag, place it in a bath of hot water and let it sit for around five mins.

Per serving: Calories: 106Kcal; Fat: 0g; Carbohydrates: 23.4g; Protein: 0g

3. Plum Jelly

Preparation time: 10 minutes **Cooking time:** 50 minutes **Servings:** 16

Ingredients:

- 5 lbs. ripe plums, slice in half & discard pits
- 6 ½ cups sugar
- 1 tbsp. butter, unsalted
- 1/75 oz. pectin
- 1 ½ cups water

Directions:

1. In a big saucepan, combine the plums and the water, and then continue to cook. Ten minutes should be spent with the lid on and simmer over medium heat.

2. Strain the plum juice by straining through a mesh strainer. Allow draining for 30 minutes. Discard plums.

3. You will get 5 ½ cups of plum juice.

4. The juice should be poured into the saucepan. Add the pectin, give it a good swirl, and then bring the mixture to a boil.

5. After adding the sugar, continue boiling the jelly for one minute.

6. Take the pot off the burner.

7. Place jelly in the sterilized jars using a ladle. Keep a headspace of a quarter of an inch. Get rid of any air bubbles.

8. Jars should have their lids on before being processed for ten minutes in a water bath that is boiling. Take the jars out of the water bath and allow them to cool down to room temperature.

9. Check seals of jars. Label and store it.

Per serving: Calories: 320Kcal; Fat: 0.8g; Carbohydrates: 83.8g; Protein: 0.2g

4. Strawberry Preserves

Preparation time: 10 minutes **Cooking time:** 20 minutes **Servings:** 10

Ingredients:

- 2 lbs. strawberries
- 2 tbsp. vinegar
- 5 cups sugar
- Pinch of salt

Directions:

1. Put all of the ingredients into the stockpot, then bring the pot to a boil.

2. Cook for 15–20 minutes while stirring the pan often.

3. Take the pot off the burner.

4. Place strawberry preserves in the jars that have been cleaned, leaving a headspace of 12 inches.

5. Get rid of any air bubbles.

6. Jars should have their lids on before being processed for ten minutes in a water bath that is boiling.

7. Take the jars out of the water bath and allow them to cool down to room temperature.

8. Check seals of jars. Label and store it properly.

Per serving: Calories: 405Kcal; Fat: 0.3g; Carbohydrates: 107g; Protein: 0.6g

5. Blueberry Preserves

Preparation time: 10 minutes **Cooking time:** 20 minutes **Servings:** 6

Ingredients:

- 6 cups blueberries
- 2 lemon juice
- 3 tbsp. pectin
- 2 cups sugar

Directions:

1. To the large pot, stir in the blueberries, then pour in the lemon juice and heat to a boil. Mixing it up frequently.

2. Mix ½-cup sugar and pectin and add it to the blueberries. Mix well, and return to boil.

3. Add remaining sugar and cook until thickens.

4. Remove pot from heat.

5. Fill the jars with blueberries, leaving 1-inch headspace. Remove air bubbles from the mixture.

6. 15 minutes in a hot water bath with lids on sealed jars.

7. Let the jars cool completely in the water bath.

8. Check seals of jars. Label and store it.

Per serving: Calories: 339Kcal; Fat: 0.5g; Carbohydrates: 88.7g; Protein: 1.1g

6. Preserved Lemons

Preparation time: 10 minutes **Cooking time:** 15 minutes **Servings:** 2

Ingredients:

- 2 lemons, rinsed, scored peel down length of lemons
- 2 tsp black peppercorns
- 2 tsp coriander seeds
- 1 cinnamon stick
- 1 bay leaf
- 3 whole cloves
- 3 cups water
- 2 tbsp. kosher salt

Directions:

1. Bring water and salt to a boil inside a pan and add lemons. Simmer for a few minutes till the lemon peel is tender enough to puncture with a knife. Reduce heat.

2. Transfer lemon to the clean canning jar. Reserve saltwater.

3. Add bay leaf, cloves, coriander seeds, cinnamon stick, and black peppercorns into the lemon jar.

4. Pour reserved saltwater over lemons, fill jar until the lemon is completely covered with saltwater.

5. Seal the jar with a lid and let it cool completely. Store in the refrigerator.

Per serving: Calories: 22Kcal; Fat: 0.2g; Carbohydrates: 6.8g; Protein: 0.9g

Chapter 16:

Salsas

1. Mango Pineapple Salsa

Preparation time: 10 minutes **Cooking time:** 30 minutes **Servings:** 4

Ingredients:

- 2 mangoes, peeled and chopped
- 2 jalapenos, chopped
- 1 sweet pepper, chopped & ½ tsp salt
- 1 onion, chopped
- 2 garlic cloves, minced
- 1 tsp ginger, grated
- ¼ cup vinegar
- ¼ cup lime juice
- 1/3 cup sugar
- 3 cups pineapple, chopped
- 1 ½ lbs. tomatoes, cored and chopped

Directions:

1. Bring all the ingredients to a boil in a big pot.

2. Simmer for ten minutes at a low temperature. Stir often to ensure even cooking.

3. Turn off the stove. Fill the jars with salsa. Allow for a half-inch headroom.

4. Jars should have lids on them to keep out air and moisture. Twenty minutes in a water bath canner is all that's required for processing.

5. Let the jars cool completely in the water bath. Check seals of jars. Label and store.

Per serving: Calories: 280Kcal; Fat: 1g; Carbohydrates: 70g; Protein: 4g

2. Simple Salsa

Preparation time: 45 minutes **Cooking time:** 30 minutes **Servings:** 3 pints

Ingredients:

- 4 cups slicing tomatoes (peeled, cored, & chopped)
- 2 cups green chilies (seeded & chopped)
- ¾ cup onions (chopped)
- ½ cup jalapeno peppers (seeded and chopped)
- 4 garlic cloves (chopped finely)
- 1 teaspoon ground cumin
- 1 tablespoon cilantro
- 1 tablespoon oregano
- 2 cups distilled white vinegar
- 1 ½ teaspoons table salt

Directions:

1. In a large pot, combine all of the above-mentioned ingredients. The saucepan should be placed on the stove and brought to a full boil while being stirred regularly to avoid burning.

2. Cook for around 20 minutes at a lower temperature before removing the pot from the stovetop. Stir often to ensure even cooking.

3. Using four jars, divide the salsa. It's important to leave about a half-inch gap on top of each container's lid for air circulation.

4. Put the covers over the containers and prepare for fifteen to twenty-five mins in a water bath canning procedure.

Per serving: Calories: 225Kcal; Fat: 9.35g; Carbohydrates: 37.18g; Protein: 9.33g

3. Zesty Salsa

Preparation time: 35 minutes **Cooking time:** 20 minutes **Servings:** 6 pints

Ingredients:

- 10 cups roughly chopped tomatoes
- 5 cups chopped and seeded bell peppers
- 5 cups chopped onions
- 2 ½ cups hot peppers, chopped, and seeded
- 1 ¼ cups cider vinegar
- 3 garlic cloves, minced
- 2 tablespoons cilantro, minced
- 3 teaspoons salt
- 1 (6 ounces) can tomato paste

Directions:

1. In a large saucepot, combine all of the ingredients with the exception of the tomato paste.

2. Simmer until the required consistency is reached.

3. Add some tomato paste and stir it in.

4. Transfer the heated salsa, leaving a headspace of 14 inches, into the hot jars.

5. Place the bowl in a warm water bath for 15 minutes.

6. One very heated salsa can be made by adding more hot peppers, while a mild salsa can be made by using fewer hot peppers. It relies on how much heat you prefer in your salsa as well as how spicy the peppers you use are.

Per serving: Calories: 142Kcal; Fat: 0.86g; Carbohydrates: 30.7g; Protein: 5.82g

4. Spicy Chunky Salsa

Preparation time: 5 minutes **Cooking time:** 15 minutes **Servings:** 3-pint jars

Ingredients:

- 6 pounds tomatoes
- 3 large green peppers, chopped
- 3 large onions, chopped
- 2 cups of white vinegar
- 1 large sweet red pepper, chopped
- 1 can (12 ounces) tomato paste
- 4 jalapeno peppers, seeded and chopped
- 2 Serrano peppers, seeded and chopped
- 1/2 cup of sugar
- 1/2 cup of minced fresh cilantro
- 1/2 cup of bottled lemon juice
- 3 garlic cloves, minced
- 4 teaspoon ground cumin
- 1 tablespoon salt
- 2 teaspoons dried oregano
- 1 teaspoon hot pepper sauce

Directions:

1. In a casserole, put the water to a boil for two and a quarter minutes. Tomatoes should be blanched for thirty to sixty seconds at a time in boiling water, one pair at one time, in a Dutch oven, using a slotted spoon.

2. Remove each tomato and immediately place it in a bowl filled with cold water. Drain the water, then dry it off with a towel. Peel the tomatoes, then coarsely chop them before

placing them in a stockpot. This will yield 9 cups of chopped tomatoes. In a separate bowl or dish, combine all of the remaining ingredients.

3. Bring an adequate amount of water to a boil before adding the ingredients. Reduce the heat to low and let the mixture cool for thirty minutes, uncovered, or until it has become somewhat thicker. The mixture should be

placed in hot jars measuring one pint, leaving a headspace of twelve inches. Eliminate any air bubbles and, if required, adjust the space by pouring hot liquid.

4. Be sure to clean the rims. Bands should be screwed on until they are fingertip tight, and lids should be centered on the jars. Place the containers inside a canner that has been filled with water and brought to a simmer. Ensure that the jars are completely submerged in the water. Bring the liquid to a simmer, and afterward keep it going at a moderate simmer for the next 15 minutes. Take the jars out of the oven and refrigerate them. Get rid of them.

Per serving: Calories: 719Kcal; Fat: 0.5g; Carbohydrates: 104.5g; Protein: 1.2g

Chapter 17:

Most Tomatoes

1. Tomato Lemon Confiture

Preparation time: 75 minutes **Cooking time:** 10 minutes **Servings:** 10-pint jars

Ingredients:

- 5 medium ripe tomatoes
- 4 cups chopped peeled tart apples
- 2 medium lemons, seeded, finely chopped

- 8 whole cloves
- 2 1/4 teaspoon ground ginger
- 6 cups sugar

Directions:

1. After being peeled, sliced, had their seeds removed, and chopped, the tomatoes were put in a strainer to drain.

2. Put the tomatoes, lemons, and apples into a Dutch oven and mix everything together. Cook while stirring for fifteen minutes at a heat setting of the medium.

3. Insert ginger and sugar. Cloves should be wrapped in cheesecloth before being added to the stew.

4. Bring the liquid to a boil. Continue stirring until all of the sugar has dissolved. Turn the heat down to a simmer and cook for forty minutes while stirring often.

5. Take the spice bag out. Leaving a headspace of 1/4 of an inch in each of nine hot sterilized

half-pint jars, carefully spoon the hot mixture into jars.

6. Eliminate any air bubbles and, if necessary, readjust the headspace by adding more hot mixture.

7. Thoroughly scrub the wheel rims. After putting the lids on the jars, screw the bands on until they are fingertip tight.

8. Put the jars you want to preserve into the canner with the boiling water, making sure that the water completely covers the jars.

9. Allow it to boil for 10 minutes.

10. Take the jars out and let them cool.

Per serving: Calories: 25Kcal; Fat: 0g; Carbohydrates: 6g; Protein: 0g

2. Spicy Tomato Jam

Preparation time: 15 minutes **Cooking time:** 1-hour **Servings:** 24

Ingredients:

- 3 pounds tomatoes
- 1 galloon boiling water
- 1 cup cider vinegar
- 1/2 cup apple juice
- 1 1/2 cups brown sugar
- 1 1/2 teaspoons salt

- 1/2 teaspoon ground black pepper
- 1/2 teaspoon ground mustard
- 1/2 teaspoon ground allspice
- 1/2 teaspoon ground cumin
- 1/4 teaspoon cayenne pepper
- 1 lemon, quartered and sliced thin

1. Make a large saucepan of tomatoes. Boiling water should be poured over the tomatoes and allowed to sit for five minutes.

2. After cooking the tomatoes, remove them with a slotted spoon and place them in ice-cold water. Remove the stems and skins.

3. In a food processor, coarsely chop the tomatoes; set any juices aside and put to the chopped tomatoes.

4. Mix cayenne pepper, cumin, allspice, mustard, black pepper, salt, apple juice, and vinegar in a large, non-reactive skillet over medium heat. Cook and stir until the sugar is completely dissolved, then stir in the diced tomatoes. Boil the mixture, then reduce the heat, cover, and boil for approximately thirty to forty-five mins, stirring frequently, or until the liquid has reduced by half. Add lemon slices and simmer for an additional 15 minutes.

5. Jars and their lids should be sterilized for at least five minutes in hot water before use. Into the sterilized, hot jars, pack the jam, filling jars to within a quarter-inch of the surface. Trace a thin spatula or knife surrounding the inner jars once having filled to get rid of any air bubbles. Using a damp paper towel, wipe jars' rims to get rid of any food residue. Put lids on top, and screw the rings on.

6. Place a rack in the bottom of a large stockpot, and fill the pot up to the halfway point with water.

7. Bring to a boil over high heat, and once boiling, use a holder to gently lower the jars into the saucepan. Keep a space of at least 2 inches between each of the jars. If necessary, add more hot water and continue adding it until the level of water is now at least one inch above the tops of the jars.

8. Once the water has reached a rolling boil, place the lid on the pot, and let the mixture cook for half an hour.

9. Take jars out of the stockpot and put them onto a wood or cloth-covered surface, a few inches apart, till cool.

10. In order to ensure that the seal is firm, press the surface of each lid with a finger, making sure the lid doesn't really bend up or down in any way. Be sure to store it someplace cool and dark.

Per serving: Calories: 52Kcal; Fat: 0.1g; Carbohydrate: 12.8g; Protein: 0.5g

3. Tomato Lemon Marmalade

Preparation time: 10 minutes **Cooking time:** 20 minutes **Servings:** 9 half-pints

Ingredients:

- 4 Cups (4 apples) chopped peeled tart apples
- 5 Medium ripe tomatoes
- 6 cups sugar
- 2 Medium seeded and finely chopped lemons
- 8 Whole cloves
- 2 1/4 Teaspoons ground ginger

Directions:

1. Prepare the tomatoes by peeling them, slicing them into quarters, and then chopping them.

2. Drain the diced tomatoes in a strainer before putting them in a Dutch oven.

3. For fifteen minutes, simmer the lemons and apples in the Dutch oven over medium heat, stirring frequently. On top of that, add a dash of ginger and a pinch of sugar.

4. Add the cloves to the mixture in a cheesecloth bag that has been tied.

5. Boil the mixture for a full two minutes, stirring often, then remove from the heat and

add the sugar. Simmer for 40 minutes at a low temperature, stirring every few minutes.

6. Pour the hot marmalade into nine warm ½-pint jars with a quarter-inch spacing and discard the spice bag.

7. Use a plastic knife to remove any air bubbles and then wipe off the rims after correcting the headspace.

8. Just enough water to cover the jars should be added to the canner. Bring the water to a boil, and then process the jars for 10 minutes.

9. Place the jars on a comfortable work surface and remove the lids. Let it sit for a while.

Per serving: Calories: 142Kcal; Fat: 0g; Carbohydrates: 36g; Protein: 0 g.

Chapter 18:

Pickles

1. Watermelon Pickles

Preparation time: 20 minutes **Cooking time:** 30 minutes **Servings:** 4 pints

Ingredients:

- 2 pounds watermelon rind
- 4 cups sugar
- 2 cups white vinegar
- 2 cups water
- 1 lemon, washed and sliced thinly
- 1 cinnamon stick
- 1 tablespoon whole cloves

Directions:

1. A cube of dark green and pink meat should be removed from the rind.

2. Combine ¼ pickling salt and 1 quart of water.

3. Heat and stir until salt is dissolved.

4. Pour saltwater over rind cubes. Leave overnight.

5. Drain and rinse cubes.

6. Place in heavy pot or kettle.

7. Drain the vegetables after they've been cooked in cold water for a few minutes.

8. A hefty saucepan should be used to mix sugar, vinegar, water, and lemon slices.

9. Place cinnamon and cloves in a cheesecloth bag and put the bag in the vinegar mixture.

10. Simmer the mixture for 10 minutes and remove the spice bag.

11. Add rind cubes to the vinegar mixture and continue cooking until cubes are translucent.

12. Put inside hot, sterile pint jars, making sure the syrup is distributed uniformly and allowing a headspace of half an inch.

13. Jars should be processed in a water bath containing boiling water for fifteen minutes.

Per serving: Calories: 70Kcal; Fat: 0g; Carbohydrates: 17g; Protein: 0g

2. Dill Pickle Spears

Preparation time: 20 minutes **Cooking time:** 30 minutes **Servings:** 7 pints

Ingredients:

- 2 gallons water
- ½ cup pickling salt
- 8 pounds pickling cucumbers, quartered lengthwise
- ½ cup mustard seeds
- 24 fresh dill sprigs
- 6 garlic cloves, halved
- 1 ½ quarts white vinegar
- 4 cups water
- ¼ cup sugar
- 2 tbsps. Pickling spice

Directions:

1. In a very large pot, combine the water and the salt while mixing to absorb the salt. After adding the cucumbers, allow the mixture to sit at room temp for a full day.

2. Put two teaspoons' worth of mustard seeds, two dill sprigs, and one clove of garlic cut in half into each sterilized jar. After draining them, split the cucumbers across the various jars.

3. In a large saucepan, combine the sugar, pickling spice, vinegar, and four cups of water and stir until the sugar is dissolved. Bring the container up to a boil, then continue cooking for another 10 minutes. Carefully pour vinegar blend into the jars, filling them to within a quarter of an inch of their utmost capacity. First, you should clean the rims of the jars, and then you should put the lids on them. They need to be processed in a bath of hot water for twenty minutes.

Per serving: Calories: 12Kcal; Fat: 0g; Carbohydrates: 1g; Protein: 0g

3. Pickled Peppers

Preparation time: 20 minutes **Cooking time:** 10 minutes **Servings:** 4 pints

Ingredients:

- 4 cups white vinegar
- 2 water cups
- 2 tablespoons sugar
- Olive oil
- 1 onion, medium diced
- 2 medium-sized carrots, medium diced
- Peppers
- Dried oregano
- Bay leaves

Directions:

1. In a saucepan of medium size, combine the sugar, water, and vinegar, and then place over medium heat till the mix achieves a boil.

2. In the meantime, sauté the carrots and onions in olive oil until the vegetables are soft.

3. Canning jars of pint-size should be used, and roughly one tablespoon of the mixture should be placed in the bottom of each jar before the peppers are added (if you prepare three small incisions on every pepper, the flavors of the brine will permeate more quickly).

4. Each jar should have one bay leaf and a half teaspoon of oregano added to it. After the jars have been sealed, they will need to be processed inside a warm water bath for ten minutes.

5. Though at least after two weeks, the flavor of these peppers will have developed to its full potential.

Per serving: Calories: 140Kcal; Fat: 1.7g; Carbohydrates: 17.59g; Protein: 1.15g

4. Jalapeno Pickles

Preparation time: 20 minutes **Cooking time:** 10 minutes **Servings:** 4 pints

Ingredients:

- 5 Jalapeno peppers, chopped
- 1 teaspoon black peppercorn
- 1 teaspoon coriander seed
- 1 tablespoon kosher salt
- 1 onion, sliced
- 2/3 cup white vinegar
- ½ cup water

Directions:

1. Put the water, coriander, salt, vinegar, and peppercorns in a pot, and bring it to a boil. After at least five minutes of cooking, take the dish off the heat. Put your jalapenos in jars made of either mason or canning glass.

2. The hot mixture should be poured over the jalapenos. Leave jars to cool at room temperature.

3. Once they have cooled, secure lids onto them and store them in the fridge.

Per serving: Calories: 4Kcal; Fat: 0g; Carbohydrates: 0g; Protein: 0.5g

5. Pickled Green Beans

Preparation time: 20 minutes **Cooking time:** 10 minutes **Servings:** 4 pints

Ingredients:

- 1¾ lbs. fresh green beans
- 1 tsp. cayenne pepper
- 4 garlic cloves, peeled
- 4 tsp. dill seed
- 2½ cups water
- 2½ cups white vinegar
- ¼ cup canning salt

Directions:

1. Put soybeans inside 4 heated 1-pint jars until there is about half an inch of space left.

2. Put garlic, dill seed, and cayenne pepper in the jars.

3. Bring the water, vinegar, and salt toward a boil in a pot that is large enough to hold all of the ingredients.

4. Carefully ladle the boiling liquid over the beans, making sure to leave a space of one-quarter of an inch at the top. Eliminate any air bubbles and, if necessary, readjust the headspace by adding more hot mixture. Thoroughly scrub the wheel rims. Put the lids on the jars, then screw the bands on until they are fingertip tight.

5. Put the jars you want to preserve into the canner with the boiling water, making sure that the water completely covers the jars. Leave it to boil for ten mins. Take the jars out and let them cool.

Per serving: Calories: 9Kcal; Fat: 0g; Carbohydrates: 2g; Protein: 1g

Chapter 19:

Relishes

1. Beet Relish

Preparation time: 15 minutes **Cooking time:** 20 minutes **Servings:** 4 pints

Ingredients:

- 1 quart chopped, cooked beets
- Quart chopped cabbage
- 1 cup chopped onion
- 1 cup chopped sweet red pepper
- 1-1/2 cup sugar
- 1 tablespoon prepared horseradish
- 1 tablespoon pickling salt
- 3 cups white vinegar

Directions:

1. Put all of the ingredients into a big saucepan. Maintain a low simmer for the next 10 minutes.

2. Stirring occasionally, now immediately pour the hot mixture into the hot jars, leaving a headspace of about a quarter of an inch. Clean the rim of the jar, then place a warm lid on top and screw it on tightly.

3. Can the food by placing this in a bath canner using water that is boiling and processing it for 15 minutes.

Per serving: Calories: 34Kcal; Fat: 0g; Carbohydrates: 8g; Protein: 0g

2. Corn Relish

Preparation time: 15 minutes **Cooking time:** 30 minutes **Servings:** 4 pints

Ingredients:

- 9 cups fresh sweet corn
- 2 cups chopped onions
- 1 cup chopped green peppers
- ½ cup chopped red peppers
- 1 cup sugar
- 2 tablespoons Salt
- 1 ½ tablespoon celery seed
- 1 ½ tablespoons mustard seed
- 1 tablespoon Turmeric
- 3 cups cider vinegar

Directions:

1. Remove kernels from the ears of corn. Peppers should have their stems, seeds, and ribs removed before use.

2. Mix together the chopped veggies, sugar, salt, and spices together with the vinegar. Bring the liquid to a boil. Cover, then bring to a simmer for 15 minutes, stirring the mixture occasionally to prevent burning.

3. Place heated relish into warm jars that have been sterilized, leaving a headspace of 14 inches. Clean the rim of the jar, then place a warm lid on top and screw it on tightly.

4. Place in a bath canner with boiling water and process for 15 minutes.

3. Amish Relish

Preparation time: 15 minutes **Cooking time:** 20 minutes **Servings:** 4 pints

Ingredients:

- 1 ½ quart finely chopped ripe tomatoes
- 1 ½ quart finely chopped green tomatoes
- 1 ½ quarts shredded cabbage
- 1 ½ quarts chopped onions
- 3 sweet red peppers, chopped

- 2 large stalks of celery, chopped
- 1 head cauliflower
- ½ cup salt
- 3 cups sugar
- 2 quarts vinegar (white or cider)

Spice bag:

- 1 teaspoon ground clove
- 1 teaspoon ground cinnamon

- 2 tablespoons mustard seed

Directions:

1. Tomatoes should have their stems and blossom ends trimmed, and celery and cauliflower should have their leaves removed. Peppers should first have their seeds and ribs removed. Process all of the vegetables in a meat grinder using a coarse blade.

2. Combine thoroughly.

3. Place the vegetables inside a large mixing bowl so that they are layered, then sprinkle 2 tablespoons of salt over each layer.

4. Allow standing for the night. First, thoroughly combine the ingredients in the morning, and then drain and squeeze out any remaining moisture.

5. Warm the vinegar with the mustard seed and sugar while the spices are in a spice bag. Bring the liquid to a boil. After adding the vegetables, bring the pot back to a boil.

6. Place heated relish inside hot jars that have been sterilized, leaving a headspace of 14 inches.

7. Clean the rim of the jar, then place a warm lid on top and screw it on tightly.

8. Place in a bath canner with boiling water and process for 15 minutes.

4. Cucumber Relish

Preparation time: 60 minutes **Cooking time:** 60 minutes **Servings:** 4-pint jars

Ingredients:

- 8 cups chopped cucumbers— blossom ends and stem removed
- 1 cup onions, chopped
- 2 cup sweet red peppers, chopped
- 2 cup sweet green peppers, chopped

- 1 tablespoon turmeric
- 1/2 cup pickling salt
- 8 cups cold water
- 2 cups brown sugar, to taste
- 4 cups white vinegar

Spice bag:

- 1 tablespoon mustard seed
- 2 medium sticks cinnamon

- 2 teaspoons whole cloves
- 2 teaspoons whole allspice

Directions:

1. Wash and dry vegetables. Peppers should have their stems, seeds, and ribs removed before being used. Prepare each veggie by chopping it and measuring it. Turmeric should be sprinkled on top.

2. Dissolve salt with water. Pour over vegetables. Leave alone for three hrs. Drain. Extra ice water should be poured over the vegetables. Allow standing for one hour. Drain well. Mix sugar and the spice bag into the vinegar. Bring to a boil by heating it. Maintain a low simmer for around ten minutes.

3. Take the spice bag out. The vegetables should be drizzled with syrup. Let stand overnight.

Bring to a boil, then remove from heat. If the dish is too dry, insert a little bit of extra vinegar into it.

4. Let the water come to a boil while stirring it to spread the heat. Put the heated condiment into the hot jars that have been sterilized, leaving a headspace of about a quarter of an inch. Clean the rim of the jar, then place a warm lid on top and screw it on tightly. Can the food by placing it in a bath canner containing water that is boiling and processing it for ten minutes.

Per serving: Calories: 318Kcal; Fat: 1g; Carbohydrates: 1g; Protein: 0g

5. Cranberry Relish

Preparation time: 15 minutes **Cooking time:** 15 minutes **Servings:** 2-pint jars

Ingredients:

- 2 cups fresh cranberries, chopped
- 6 Medjool dates, pitted and chopped
- 1/2 shallot, finely diced
- 1 orange, seeded and chopped
- 4 sage leaves, finely chopped
- 2 tablespoons brown sugar
- 1 cup red wine vinegar
- 1/4 cup sugar
- 1 tablespoon salt

Directions:

1. Place the cranberries, dates, shallots, sage leaves, and orange segments in a medium bowl. Toss everything thoroughly to incorporate, and then put the bowl to the side.

2. In a small saucepan set above moderate to high heat, combine the sugar and salt with the vinegar, and then bring to a boil. Adjust the temperature so that it maintains a simmer for ten minutes, then take it off the heat.

3. Scoop the cranberry relish three-quarter way into the storage cans and top with the vinegar mixture, leaving 1/4inch head space.

4. Tightly seal the cans and place them in a 15-minute water bath and let them cool in a dry place.

Per serving: Calories: 81Kcal; Fat: 0.1g; Carbohydrates: 21.6g; Protein: 0.6g

Chapter 20:

Chutneys

1. Mango Chutney

Preparation time: 15 minutes **Cooking time:** 45 minutes **Servings:** 4-pint jars

Ingredients:

- 6 cups sliced green mangos
- 1/2 lb. fresh ginger
- 3 1/2 cups currants
- 8 cups sugar
- 2 cups vinegar
- 3 cups ground cayenne pepper
- 1 cup salt

Directions:

1. After peeling it, cut the ginger in half. Thin slices should be taken from half of the ginger, while the remaining ginger should be chopped up into larger pieces.

2. Make a fine powder out of the sliced ginger and 1/2 of currants by pulverizing them together in a blender. Everything save the mangoes should be placed in a pot.

3. Cook for 15 minutes over a heat setting of the medium. In the meantime, prepare the six cups by cutting, halving, pitting, and slicing the green mangoes.

4. After the first fifteen mins of cooking, connect the mangoes and continue cooking over medium heat for an additional 30 minutes, or until the mangoes are soft.

5. After pouring into shot glasses, wipe the rims clean and then secure the caps and rings with the included screws.

6. Make use of the procedure of putting the jars in hot water for ten minutes; this goes for both pints and quarts.

Per serving: Calories: 37Kcal; Fat: 0g; Carbohydrates: 12g; Protein: 0g

2. Rhubarb Cherry Chutney

Preparation time: 15 minutes **Cooking time:** 35 minutes **Servings:** 6-pint jars

Ingredients:

- 2 lbs. chopped fresh rhubarb
- 2 cups chopped cherries
- 1 chopped apple
- 1 chopped red onion
- 1 chopped celery rib
- 3 minced garlic cloves
- 1 tbsp. chopped crystallized ginger
- 2 cups brown sugar
- 1 cup red wine vinegar
- 3/4 tsp. ground cinnamon
- 1/2 tsp. ground coriander
- 1/4 tsp. ground cloves

Directions:

1. Put all of the ingredients into a stockpot that has a capacity of 6 quarts and bring them to a boil. Simmer for 30 minutes while uncovered.

2. Transfer to covered containers. If freezing, use freezer-safe containers and fill to within ½ inch of the tops.

3. You can keep it in the freezer for up to a year or in the refrigerator for up to three weeks. The frozen salsa should be defrosted in the refrigerator before being served.

Per serving: Calories: 102Kcal; Fat: 0g; Carbohydrates: 27g; Protein: 0g.

3. Garlicky Lime Chutney

Preparation time: 10 minutes **Cooking time:** 60 minutes **Servings:** 3-pint jars

Ingredients:

- 12 limes, scrubbed and cut into 1/2-inch dice
- 12 garlic cloves, thinly sliced lengthwise
- 1 (4-inch) piece fresh ginger, peeled and thinly sliced
- 3/4 cup sugar
- 8 green chili peppers (jalapeños or Serrano's), stemmed, seeded, and thinly sliced
- 1 tablespoon chili powder
- 1 cup distilled white vinegar

Directions:

1. Prepare a hot water bath. Bring the jars in it to keep warm. After washing them in hot, soapy water, the rings and lids can be placed aside to dry.

2. Mix the lemons, garlic, ginger, chilies, and chili powder in a medium saucepan. Give everything a good stir, and then bring the mixture up to a simmer.

3. After adding the vinegar and sugar, reduce the heat to a simmer and continue cooking, stirring periodically, for around seventy minutes, or until the limes are fork soft and the sauce is thick enough to mound once spilled out of a spoon. Take the dish away from the heat.

4. Place the chutney in the jars that have been prepped, leaving a headspace of about a quarter of an inch. To pop any air bubbles, you'll need to use a tool that's not made of metal. Remove any debris from the rims, then secure both the lids and rings.

5. Put the jars into a bath of hot water and let them sit there for twenty minutes. Turn off the stove and leave the jars to cool in the water bath for a while.

6. Remove the containers first from the canner that contains hot water as carefully as possible. Placed to the side to chill for a period of 12 hours.

7. Make sure the lids have good seals on them. Take off the rings, clean the jars, label them with the current date, and put them away in a cabinet or a pantry.

8. For the best flavor, allow the chutney to rest for 3 days before serving. Set in the refrigerator any jars that don't seal properly, and use them within 6 weeks. Properly secure jars will last in the cupboard for twelve months. Once the package has been opened, store it in the refrigerator and use it within a month.

Per serving: Calories: 58Kcal; Fat: 1g; Carbohydrates: 12g; Protein: 0g

4. Cilantro Chutney

Preparation time: 45 minutes **Cooking time:** 10 minutes **Servings:** 5-pint jars

Ingredients:

- 1/2 cup of yogurt (this can be omitted or replaced with a vegan-based version of yogurt)
- Lemon juice, three tablespoons
- Cilantro with stems removed (small branches can be left intact), one bunch
- Mint leaves, about one cup packed
- Ginger, sliced (2 teaspoons)
- Sea salt, 1/2 teaspoon
- One garlic clove
- One medium-sized jalapeno, sliced finely
- Sugar, 1/2 teaspoon

Directions:

1. Put all of the ingredients listed above into a blender and add 1 tbsp. of water. Blend until smooth.

2. After tasting it, add extra seasoning if you feel it needs it, and then transfer it to a sterile jar so it can be kept in the refrigerator. If you want to substitute the yogurt for a non-dairy alternative, you can add coconut or soy-based yogurt. Tofu is another option to consider.

3. If you wish to preserve for a longer period, omit the yogurt entirely and store the chutney in a jar for up to one month in your refrigerator.

Per serving: Calories: 88Kcal; Fat: 0g; Carbohydrates: 22g; Protein: 1g

Chapter 21:
Sauces

1. Brazilian Fish Sauce

Preparation time: 10 minutes **Cooking time:** 50 minutes **Servings:** 3

Ingredients:

- 3 tablespoons lime juice
- 1 tablespoon ground cumin
- 1 tablespoon paprika
- 2 teaspoons minced garlic
- 1 teaspoon salt
- 1 teaspoon ground black pepper
- 1 ½ pound tilapia fillets, cut into chunks
- 2 tablespoons olive oil
- 2 onions, chopped
- 4 large bell peppers, sliced
- 1 (16-ounce) can diced tomatoes, drained
- 1 (16-ounce) can of coconut milk
- 1 bunch fresh cilantro, chopped (optional)

Directions:

1. Lime juice, black pepper, kosher salt, ground cumin, paprika, and smoked paprika should be combined in a bowl. After adding the tilapia, give everything a good mix to ensure it is evenly coated.

2. Place the lid on the bowl, and place it in the refrigerator for twenty mins and up to 24 hours.

3. In a large pot, bring the olive oil to a simmer over medium-high heat. Once the oil is hot, add the onions and stir-fry them for one to two minutes. Turn the temperature down to medium.

4. The saucepan should have successive layers of chopped tomatoes, bell peppers, and fish placed inside of it. Over the top of the existing mixture, add some coconut milk.

5. The saucepan should be covered and allowed to cook for fifteen mins with frequent stirring.

6. After mixing in the cilantro, continue cooking for another 5 to 10 minutes, or until the tilapia is done cooking all the way through.

Per serving: Calories:359Kcal; Fat:21.8g; Carbohydrate: 15.6g; Protein: 27.4g

2. Easy Tomato Sauce

Preparation time: 10 minutes **Cooking time:** 15 minutes **Servings:** 3

Ingredients:

- 4 tablespoons olive oil
- 1 onion, chopped
- 3 tomatoes, chopped
- 1 tablespoon tomato puree
- Salt and pepper to taste

Directions:

1. Cook the onions in a big pan with the olive oil until they are transparent, which should take around 15 minutes.

2. After the fluids have begun to thicken, add the tomatoes and continue to cook. Mix in the pepper, salt, and purée while stirring.

3. Reduce the heat, then cover the pot and let it boil for another fifteen mins, or until it has reached the desired consistency.

Per serving: Calories: 204Kcal; Fat: 16g; Carbohydrate: 14.8g; Protein: 2.2g

Chapter 22:

Vinegars

1. Apple Cider Vinegar

Preparation time: 20 minutes   **Cooking time:** 0 minutes **Servings:** 2 liters

Ingredients:

- 10 apples
- 2 sterilized glass bowls one larger than the other
- Cheesecloth

Instructions:

1. Apples should be well washed and then sliced into quarters. You do not need to remove the peel or seeds.

2. Leave the apples to air and turn brown, for up to 1 hour. Place the apples in the smaller bowl and fill with just enough water to fully cover them.

3. Place the bowl in a spot that is warm and dark where it will not be disturbed for the next six months with the cheesecloth tightly covering the top.

4. An airing cupboard or hot water cupboard is ideal. It is common for a grayish or brown scum to grow on the surface of the liquid, do not worry about this unless it is white, green, or black and is powdery or fuzzy in appearance. If the apple cider vinegar has grown mold you must discard the entire batch and start over.

5. After the fermentation has gone on for six months, scrape out the scum, pour the fluid thru a coffee grinder together into a new clean bowl, and then cover the bowl with a cheesecloth and let it sit for another four to six weeks. Apple cider vinegar will last for up to a year.

Per serving: Calories: 25Kcal; Fat: 0.2g; Carbohydrates: 15.4g; Protein: 0.3g.

2. Raspberry Vinegar

Preparation time: 35 minutes **Cooking time:** 0 **Servings:** 1 cup

Ingredients:

- 1-pint ripe raspberries
- 1 cup red wine vinegar

Directions:

1. Place entire raspberries in a jar that holds a pint of liquid and carefully pack them in so that they take up as little space as possible. Pour in enough vinegar to cover the raspberries. Allow macerating with a cover for a week at room temperature.

2. Place a strainer on a medium bowl; use a double layer of cheesecloth to the line. Strain vinegar mixture through a strainer. Pull the edges of the cheesecloth together and squeeze it to release the fluids until the juices begin to pour from the cheesecloth and become thicker.

3. Remove cheesecloth along with solids. Add vinegar to a clean 8-oz. jar or bottle. Chill with a cover-up to 6 months.

Per serving: Calories: 222Kcal; Fat: 0g; Carbohydrate: 49g; Protein: 5g

3. Lemongrass Vinegar

Preparation time: 20 minutes **Cooking time:** 0 minutes **Servings:** 2 cups

Ingredients

- 3 stalks lemongrass
- 2 cups rice vinegar

Directions:

1. Lemongrass stalks should be sliced very thinly along the bottom eight inches, and the slices should be placed in a very clean one-quart glass jar before being crushed with a wooden spoon.

2. After adding the vinegar, let the mixture steep in a dark, cold area for at least four days and up to two weeks, depending on how potent you want the flavor to be while keeping the mixture covered with a lid.

3. Pour the vinegar that has been strained into the glass pitcher via a fine-mesh sieve. Dispose of the lemongrass that has been sliced.

4. Transfer mixture to two extremely clean half-pint glass jars, and cover each jar with its respective lid.

Per serving: Calories: 73Kcal; Fat: 0g; Carbohydrates: 8g; Protein: 1g

4. Chipotle Vinegar

Preparation time: 20 minutes **Cooking time:** 5 minutes **Servings:** 2 cups

Ingredients:

- 2-3 chipotle chilis, stemmed, halved, and seeded
- 2 ½ cups Spanish sherry vinegar

Directions:

1. In a small saucepan, char the chipotle peppers for two minutes over medium heat.

2. After adding the vinegar, continue to cook for another two to three minutes.

3. Remove from the heat and place in a container with a tight-fitting lid.

4. Let vinegar rest for no shorter than 24 hours before using it.

5. If you store this vinegar in a cold, dark place, it will be ready for use in about six months.

Per serving: Calories: 52Kcal; Fat: 0g; Carbohydrates: 4g; Protein: 1g

Chapter 23:

Condiments

1. Berry Syrup

Preparation time: 60 minutes **Cooking time:** 25 minutes **Servings:** 9 half-pints

Ingredients:

- 6 ½ cups fresh berries
- 6 ¾ cups of sugar

Directions:

1. In a pan, add washed berries and crush them.

2. Allow it to boil, then reduce the heat to a simmer for 5–10 minutes.

3. Strain in a sieve and collect the juice. Do not use the pulp.

4. Mix the juice with sugar (6 ¾ cups) and let it boil; simmer for 60 seconds.

5. Turn the heat off.

6. In sterilized hot jars, add the mixture, and leave half-inch space from above. Take care to eliminate any air bubbles. After cleaning the rim of the jar, replace the lid and secure it with the bands (do not screw too tightly).

7. Boil as per your altitude.

8. Take the jars out and cool for 12 to 24 hours, and the lid should not pop down or up. Keep in a cool, dry, and dark place.

Per serving: Calories: 92Kcal; Fat: 0g Carbohydrates: 21g; Protein: 3g

2. Garlic Dill Pickles

Preparation time: 1 hour **Cooking time:** 15 minutes **Servings:** 4

Ingredients:

- 3 lbs. cucumbers
- 1½ cups apple cider vinegar
- 1 tsp. red chili flake
- 2 tsp. black peppercorns
- 4 tsp. dill seed
- 8 peeled garlic cloves
- 2 tbsps. pickling salt
- 1½ cups water

Directions:

1. Wash and dry cucumbers, and cut them into spears. Remove the blossom end of the cucumbers.

2. To make the brine, mix equal parts vinegar, water, and salt together in a saucepan. Over medium-high heat, bring the liquid to a boil. Equally divide the dill seed, garlic cloves, red chili flakes, and black peppercorns between the jars.

3. Cucumbers should be packed into the canning containers as snugly as possible without being crushed in the process. The brine should be poured over the cucumbers, and the jars should be filled to within a quarter of an inch of the top.

4. Tap the jars to assist in the removal of air bubbles. Clean the rims of the jars, and then screw the lids on tightly. Add the jars to the canning pot and boil for 15 minutes.

5. Once the jars have cooled, place them in the fridge.

6. Let the pickles sit for at least one week before eating.

Per serving: Calories 5Kcal; Fat: 0g; Carbohydrates: 12g; Protein: 0g

3. Garlic Tomato Sauce

Preparation time: 65 minutes **Cooking time:** 2 hours 35 minutes **Servings:** 4 pints

Ingredients:

- 15 pounds tomatoes
- 8 garlic cloves, thinly sliced
- 2 tablespoons red pepper flakes

- 3 bay leaves
- 1/3 cup olive oil
- 4 tablespoons bottled lemon juice

Directions:

1. If you desire a smooth sauce, either use a food mill to peel your tomatoes, or blanch and peel your tomatoes the old-fashioned way (see here).

2. Core the peeled tomatoes and coarsely chop. Set aside.

3. Garlic, dried red pepper seasoning, bay leaves, and oil should be mixed together in a large stockpot and placed over medium-high to high heat. Wait 5 minutes before serving.

4. After the tomatoes have been chopped, put them in the pot and keep the water to a boil. Cook for one and a half to two hours, stirring the mixture occasionally until the tomatoes have completely broken down and become soft. Turn off the heat and pass the cooked tomatoes through a food mill. This should leave you with a smooth sauce. In the event that you do not have access to a food mill, you can puree the tomatoes in a mixing bowl by working in batches until they reach the desired consistency.

5. Place the pot back on the stove over a medium-high heat setting, then add the sauce. Cook for around thirty minutes, or until the sauce has reached the desired consistency (you do not need a hard boil, but lots of steam coming out is great).

6. Prepare 4-pint jars and your water bath canner, but add extra water to the canner so the jars are covered by 2 inches to account for the long processing time.

7. After the jars have been prepared, add one tablespoon of lemon juice to each one. Place the tomato sauce in the jars using a ladle, making sure to leave a headspace of half an inch.

8. The directions for water bath canning state that any air bubbles should be removed, the rims of the jars should be cleaned, the lids should be finger-tight, and the jars should be processed for 35 minutes.

Per serving: Calories 246Kcal; Fat 4.8g; Carbohydrate 42 g; Protein 3.3 g

Conclusion

You might be feeling a little overwhelmed after reading all of this. Do not be alarmed; this is completely normal because there is so much to take in. This book was not written to frighten you or make you feel inept. No, if anything, this book was written to help you navigate the difficulties that home canning may present.

Canning your own food is a gratifying hobby. When you look at your canned foods and realize you were able to do it on your own, it will provide you with the motivation you need to make this a regular habit. Suppose you regularly can your food. You will notice a decrease in the amount of money you spend on produce and other canned foods. Home canning will also have a positive impact on your eating habits. The foods you preserve will be far healthier than the preserved foods sold in supermarkets.

Once you have mastered the art of canning your food, you will be unstoppable! I won't lie to you and tell you everything will be simple – especially the first few times. You will make a few mistakes and may make a mess of your kitchen. This is to be expected; you are, after all, a beginner.

However, as time passes, the number of errors you make will decrease, and you will no longer require the assistance of this guide. You will be able to create unique recipes! This has to begin with the first steps, which include giving this book a shot.

I hope this book was able to teach you the fundamentals of food canning and preservation. I hope this book clearly explains the various concepts and rules associated with canning and preserving food. In addition, I hope you can follow all of the instructions in this book.

The next step is to put everything you have learned from this book into practice. Remember that knowledge is meaningless unless it is put to use. Look for canning and preservation recipes online or in books, and then try them out for yourself. Just make sure that you always remember the reminders, especially the fact that you must first understand the method that you are going to use before you begin doing anything.

Thank you, and best wishes!

Index

Made in the USA
Las Vegas, NV
05 May 2023

71559369R00044